minutemeals
vegetarian

inventive, satisfying everyday meals

Edited by Evie Righter

Wiley Publishing, Inc.

ISBN: 0-7645-6608-3

Cataloging-in-Publication Data is available upon request from the Library of Congress.

minutemeals

Joe Langhan, President, minutemeals.com Inc.

Miriam Garron, Managing Editor

Miriam Rubin, Consulting Food Editor

Cover design by Edwin Kuo

Interior design by Edwin Kuo

Cover photograph by David Bishop

Manufactured in the United States of America

10   9   8   7   6   5   4   3   2   1

welcome to *minutemeals vegetarian*.

You may already know our 20-minute homecooked menus from our web site, minutemeals.com, or you may, in fact, cook from the 150 menus in our recently published flagship book, *minutemeals*. If this is a first meeting, let us introduce ourselves and explain why we feel sure that our simple menu concept, quick home-cooking, will benefit your life quantifiably and in so doing improve your family's lives as well.

the tempo of life, as we all know too well, has accelerated. There are more things to do and less time to do them in, and as the saying goes, something had to give. One was the family meal. The very notion now seems almost anachronistic. Even if there were the time to shop for it and cook it, who would sit down to eat it? No two schedules are alike. The solution: Eat on the run, or order in, or snack round the clock.

the solutions are quick fixes at best, though. The family meal, it turns out, is important to the day. For many people, it is the only time-out— a chance to meet, greet, regroup, connect. To say nothing of how pivotal it is nutritionally. For some working parents, dinnertime is the one opportunity over the course of a day to monitor what their children eat. A homecooked meal goes way beyond what appears on the plate.

enter minutemeals—a way for the homemaker to get back to basics, to prepare a full-course menu, but in only 20 minutes. How is that possible? We've done as much of the organizing, the legwork, as possible so that you can concentrate on preparing the meal. We provide the menu, the shopping list of main ingredients, the list of staples you will need for that menu from your pantry, and a gameplan—the steps we took when we developed the menu that insure its completion in 20 minutes. We know the system works from the repeated glowing feedback on our web site.

user feedback, in fact, inspired these vegetarian menus, each developed by a culinary professional with an eye to overall nutritional content, not always a given when it comes to vegetarian cooking. Eighty minutemeal menus follow. Try out our concept. Taste our cooking. Enjoy. The return on investment is incalculable when you cook the minutemeals way.

Evie Righter, *Editor*

minutemeals
vegetarian

meet the minutemeals chefs

We'd like you to meet the chefs behind minutemeals, the people whose creativity and ingenuity created the delicious menus in this book. Their combined expertise is our ace in the hole—the secret that keeps our menus fresh, interesting, and full of great ideas. You'll find their helpful comments throughout the book, paired with the menus they created.

Nancy Allen

Amanda Cushman

Ruth Fisher

Miriam Garron

Joanne Hayes

Marge Perry

Paul Piccuito

Miriam Rubin

Hillary Davis Tonken

how to use this book

minutemeals vegetarian is designed to be as efficient as possible. Twenty minutes, after all, is a short amount of time to cook a full meal and place it on the table. For you to be able to do the cooking with as few setbacks as possible, we took care of as many of the time-consuming details as we could to insure your success. Rely on our system and you will have a delicious dinner on the table in 20 minutes.

Each menu includes a shopping list of the major ingredients needed, as well as a complete list of ingredients we consider standard pantry items. No more hunting through multiple recipes to glean what you need to buy on the way home—we've done that for you. Our "menu gameplan" then orders the sequence of just how to go about cooking the meal—what dish needs to be started first, what should follow, and so on. We've also noted when to preheat the oven or broiler so that it will be sufficiently heated for maximum cooking results. The double-page format of each menu guarantees that when you refer to the cooking directions of any given dish you are always on the "same page."

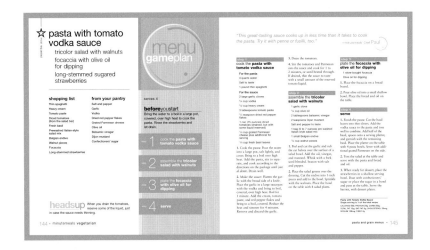

This book offers 80 tempting vegetarian menus. Vegetarian is a popular category on our web site and we know these menus will be a hit. New ideas and fresh flavors make these vegetarian menus appealing, as well as fast. In addition we've highlighted which of the menus have scored as "☆ most requested" on our web site.

The minutemeals clock starts ticking when you put the ingredients for a menu on the kitchen counter. The first several times you make a menu expect it to take a few minutes more than you had anticipated: the system itself and the recipes are new to you and, as the saying goes, practice makes perfect. Once you've had the practice, we know that you will find the results delicious . . . and quick.

quick tips from the pros

mollie katzen

make healthy convenience foods

at my farmers' market I buy organic, locally grown fruits and vegetables in bulk. I don't have enough room to store all that fresh produce, so I've come up with some simple ways to preserve it for a variety of quick uses. (No farmers' market? Try to buy produce grown in the US, which has stricter pesticide limits than many other countries.) Here are a few of my favorite tricks:

separate strawberries, raspberries, or peach slices on sheet pans and freeze 30 minutes. Transfer to self-sealing freezer bags, label, and stack in the freezer. (Freeze serving-size portions for added convenience.) I use them straight from the freezer, pureed with fruit juice or yogurt in the blender. Or, I defrost and drain some fruit, and then spread it on toast or muffins, lightly sweetened if necessary. By using the produce raw, I get vitamins or minerals that may be lost in the cooking process.

partially-cooked vegetables retain their shape and texture when frozen and defrosted, so I parboil chopped vegetables like broccoli or cauliflower before packing them into self-sealing freezer bags. Again, I pack them in "serving-size" portions, so that they are ready for stir-fries, to add to pasta, or just to heat briefly in the microwave.

With close to 5 million books in print, including her classic *Moosewood Cookbook,* Mollie Katzen is one of the *New York Times'* ten best-selling cookbook authors of all time. Her other books include *The Enchanted Broccoli Forest* and, for children, the award-winning *Pretend Soup* and its sequel, *Honest Pretzels.* A charter member of the Harvard School of Public Health Nutrition Roundtable, and named by *Health Magazine* as one of the "Five Women Who Changed the Way We Eat," Mollie is widely credited with bringing healthful cooking to mainstream dinner tables. Since 1995 she has been the host of *Mollie Katzen's Cooking Show* on public television.

curtis aikens

vegetarian flavor boosts

get the maximum flavor from chopped vegetables by "sweating"—cooking them over low heat, covered, in a bit of oil, butter, or stock so that they release their juices without browning. Speed up the process by adding a bit of salt at the beginning—it draws out the juices. Use the vegetables as the base for a quick soup or stew.

when I'm short on time and crave homemade soup I juice 2 bunches of celery (yep—I bought a juicer last century!) and heat the juice with a little butter, salt and pepper. If you don't have a juicer, puree the celery in a food processor or blender and strain out the pulp.

make double batches of vegetable chili, stew, or side dishes, fold cooked rice into the leftovers, and then roll it into flour tortillas or spoon it into taco shells.

lay a thick slice of multi-grain bread under hot soup or stew. It soaks up the sauce and gives a meaty, main-dish feel to even simple vegetable dishes, and saves you from cooking a side dish.

my mama's cornbread accompanies many meals in my house, but always in a different form. Dress up a prepared mix with hot peppers or cayenne, cheese, fresh or dried herbs—whatever you have on hand.

Curtis Aikens has been with Food Network since its inception and currently hosts its program *Calling All Cooks*. He has also appeared on *The Oprah Winfrey Show*, *The Home Show*, CNN, *Good Morning America* and *Entertainment Tonight*. His books include *Curtis Aikens' Guide to the Harvest* and *Curtis Cooks with Heart & Soul*. Curtis has worked as a food consultant to the U.S. Open, New York City's Plaza Hotel, the UN cafeteria, and many other restaurants and markets. Inspired by his struggle to overcome adult illiteracy, Curtis devotes time and money to adult literacy programs across the country.

didi emmons

faster and prettier

i love using paper-thin slices of cabbage, onions, daikon, carrots, apples, celery, and other vegetables. They are great raw in fresh slaws, springroll and tortilla fillings. And since they cook in no time, they are perfect for stir-fries and roasted dishes, too. The plastic slicers sold at Asian markets cut foods thinner and faster than an Iron Chef ever could, and are a fraction of the price of the bulky stainless mandolines used in French kitchens (the blade seems to stay sharper longer, too). Be sure to use the guard when slicing—these slicers can slice through fingers, too.

eye-appeal can make the simplest foods more enticing: A crudite basket gives plain vegetables a chance to dazzle. Choose a small variety of vegetables and an attractive bowl or basket, *not* a platter. Broccoli, green beans, carrots, etc., look better when they are hugging each other, but on a platter everything just lays there flat. It's like the difference between flowers lying on a table versus standing in a vase. Clump the veggies with their own kind—broccoli in one bunch, red pepper strips in another, etc., to create patches of color and texture.

i often substitute lentils in a recipe calling for dried beans, because they cook in just 25 minutes. One of my favorite simple meals consists of brown or French lentils, rinsed with cold water and tossed with a simple vinaigrette. Then I add things that don't need chopping—like raisins, toasted nuts, or even prechopped sun-dried tomatoes.

Didi Emmons is the author of *Vegetarian Planet* (Harvard Common Press 1997) and is the chef/owner of Veggie Planet in Cambridge, Massachusetts. Her second book, *Down to Earth Entertaining for a Vegetarian Planet,* will be published by Houghton Mifflin in 2003.

minute

chapter 1

sandwiches and pizzas

meals
vegetarian

grilled cheese sandwiches
with avocado and sun-dried tomato
tomato wedges with pesto
chilled plums and nectarines

menu
gameplan

serves 4

step **1** make the **grilled cheese sandwiches**

step **2** while the **sandwiches** toast, prepare the **tomatoes**

step **3** prepare the **plums and nectarines**

step **4** **serve**

shopping list

Whole-grain or country-style bread

Ripe avocado, preferably Haas

Pre-shredded quick-melt Cheddar cheese (chef's style)

Sliced oil-packed sun-dried tomatoes

Prepared pesto

Vine-ripe tomatoes

Ripe, red plums, ripe nectarines or peaches

from your pantry

Butter

Vinaigrette dressing, store-bought

Pepper

 Finding a ripe avocado in the market can be difficult. Frequently, most are rock hard.

To ripen an avocado, hold it at room temperature, turning it, for several days (or longer), until it yields when gently pressed.

"I love to make these sandwiches on a cast-iron grill pan, which can be found in most hardware or kitchenware stores for under $15."

—minutemeals' Chef Paul

step 1

make the **grilled cheese sandwiches with avocado and sun-dried tomato**

8 slices whole-grain or country-style bread

2 tablespoons butter, at room temperature

1 ripe avocado, preferably Haas

About 1 cup pre-shredded quick-melt Cheddar cheese

8 teaspoons sliced oil-packed sun-dried tomatoes

1. Place the bread slices on a sheet of waxed paper or a cutting board. Spread one side of each slice with butter. Turn over 4 of the slices.

2. Cut the avocado in half, remove the pit, and peel; cut each half into 8 slices.

3. Preheat a grill pan, if using, or a large nonstick skillet over medium-low heat.

4. Place 3 tablespoons (scant ¼ cup) of cheese on each of the 4 unbuttered slices of bread. Top the cheese with 2 teaspoons sun-dried tomato slices.

Arrange 4 slices of avocado over the tomato slices, then sprinkle on the remaining 1 tablespoon cheese. Top each with a slice of bread, butter side up.

5. Place the sandwiches in the heated grill pan and cook for 5 to 7 minutes per side, or until toasted and golden.

step 2

while the **sandwiches** toast, prepare the **tomato wedges with pesto**

3 tablespoons prepared pesto

2 tablespoons vinaigrette dressing

6 medium, vine-ripe tomatoes

Pepper to taste

1. Combine the pesto and vinaigrette in a medium serving bowl.

2. Rinse the tomatoes, pat dry, and cut into thin wedges. Add to the bowl, tossing to coat, and season with pepper. Place the bowl on the table.

step 3

prepare the **plums and nectarines**

Ripe red plums

Ripe nectarines or peaches

Rinse the plums and nectarines in a colander. Chill in the colander until serving time.

step 4

serve

1. Remove the sandwiches when done and place on a cutting board. Cut in half and place on a serving platter or individual plates. Serve with the tomato wedges.

2. When ready for dessert, transfer plums and nectarines to a serving bowl and serve with dessert plates.

Grilled Cheese Sandwiches with Avocado and Sun-Dried Tomato
Single serving is ¼ of the total recipe
CALORIES 415; PROTEIN 14g; CARBS 35g; TOTAL FAT 25g; SAT FAT 11g; CHOLESTEROL 45mg; SODIUM 471mg; FIBER 7g

portobello reubens

broccoli slaw
potato salad
rice pudding with raspberries

serves 4

shopping list

Portobello mushroom caps, stems removed (from the produce department)

Organic sauerkraut

Swiss cheese, thinly sliced

Thousand Island dressing

Broccoli cole slaw (bagged, from the produce department)

Chopped scallions (from the salad bar)

Slaw dressing or ranch dressing

Lemon juice or vinegar

Potato salad, preferably French style (from the deli counter or prepared foods section)

Rice pudding (from the refrigerated prepared foods section)

Quick-thaw frozen raspberries

from your pantry

Olive oil

Salt and pepper

Paprika

beforeyoustart

Preheat the broiler. Thaw the frozen raspberries according to the directions on the package.

step 1 make the **portobello reubens**

step 2 prepare the **broccoli slaw**

step 3 plate the **potato salad**

step 4 **serve**

 If you don't have Thousand Island dressing among the staples in your refrigerator, make your own: Stir ketchup and chopped pickle into reduced-fat or regular mayonnaise. Or simpler still, use chili sauce in place of the ketchup and pickle.

"The question here isn't 'where's the beef?' but 'where's the rye bread?' With portobello mushrooms, you really don't need any bread."

—minutemeals' Chef Nancy

step 1

make the **portobello reubens**

4 large portobello mushroom caps, stems removed

2 tablespoons olive oil

Salt and pepper to taste

3/4 cup drained organic sauerkraut

6 ounces thinly sliced Swiss cheese

2 tablespoons store-bought Thousand Island dressing

1. Preheat the broiler.

2. Brush the mushroom caps on both sides with the olive oil and season with salt and pepper. Place them, open side down, on the broiler pan rack. Broil about 4 inches from the heat about 5 minutes. Turn and broil the second side for 2 to 3 minutes, or until tender.

3. Meanwhile, rinse and drain the sauerkraut. With your hands, squeeze out as much water as possible from the sauerkraut.

4. Turn the mushrooms open side up. Fill each cap with some of the sauerkraut and top it with some of the Swiss cheese. Broil for 1 to 2 minutes, or until the cheese is melted and the sauerkraut is hot. Transfer each mushroom cap to a plate and spoon 1/2 tablespoon of the Thousand Island dressing over each.

step 2

prepare the **broccoli slaw**

1 bag (16 ounces) broccoli cole slaw

1/4 cup chopped scallions

2 tablespoons store-bought slaw dressing or ranch dressing

Fresh lemon juice or vinegar to taste

Salt and pepper to taste

In a salad bowl, combine the broccoli slaw, scallions, dressing, lemon juice or vinegar, and salt and pepper and toss to mix. Place the bowl on the table.

step 3

plate the **potato salad**

1 pound store-bought potato salad, preferably French style

Paprika for garnish

Transfer the potato salad to a serving bowl and sprinkle with paprika. Place the bowl on the table.

step 4

serve

1. Serve the mushrooms with the salads alongside.

2. When ready for dessert, spoon the rice pudding into 4 dessert bowls and top each with some of the raspberries and any juice that has collected as they melted.

Portobello Reubens
Single serving is 1/4 of the total recipe
CALORIES 319; PROTEIN 17g; CARBS 13g; TOTAL FAT 23g; SAT FAT 9g; CHOLESTEROL 39mg; SODIUM 428mg; FIBER 3g

tomato and avocado egg-salad sandwiches

vegetable chips
savory carrot salad
lemon sorbet with blueberries

shopping list

Cilantro leaves

Shredded carrots
(from the salad bar or from
the produce department)

Lemon (for juice)

Peeled hard-cooked eggs
(from the salad bar)

Ripe avocado, preferably
Haas

Plum tomato

Small pimiento-stuffed green
salad olives

Whole-grain bread

Spinach leaves

Vegetable chips

Lemon sorbet

Fresh blueberries

from your pantry

Olive oil

Ground cumin

Salt and pepper

Light or regular mayonnaise

serves 4

beforeyoustart

Pick over and rinse the blueberries in a colander; let drain until serving time.

| step | 1 | assemble the **savory carrot salad** |

| step | 2 | make the **sandwiches** |

| step | 3 | **serve** |

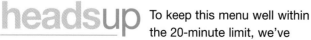 **heads**up To keep this menu well within the 20-minute limit, we've suggested buying hard-cooked eggs at the salad bar in the supermarket. They, of course, have the advantage of being ready-to-use.

"It really takes very little additional effort and time to turn plain egg salad into something special. Tomato, olives, and avocado did the trick here."

—minutemeals' Chef Paul

step 1

assemble the **savory carrot salad**

- 1/3 cup cilantro leaves
- 3 cups shredded carrots
- 1 tablespoon fresh lemon juice (1/2 lemon)
- 1 tablespoon olive oil
- Pinch of ground cumin
- Salt and pepper to taste

Rinse the cilantro sprigs and pat dry. Remove enough leaves to measure 1/3 cup and place in a medium bowl. Add the carrots, lemon juice, olive oil, cumin, and salt and pepper. Toss to combine. Place the bowl on the table.

step 2

make the **tomato and avocado egg-salad sandwiches**

- 6 peeled hard-cooked eggs
- 1 small ripe avocado, preferably Haas
- 1 plum tomato
- 1/4 cup small pimiento-stuffed green salad olives
- 1/3 cup light or regular mayonnaise
- Salt and pepper to taste
- 8 slices whole-grain bread
- 4 to 6 small spinach leaves

1. Make the egg salad: Place the eggs in a medium bowl and chop with a pastry blender or fork.

2. Cut the avocado in half and remove the pit. Cut the flesh (still in the peel) into cubes. Scoop out with a spoon into the bowl.

3. Dice the plum tomato. Add it to the bowl with the olives, mayonnaise, and salt and pepper. Mix well.

4. Assemble the sandwiches: Lay the bread slices on the work surface. Place spinach leaves on half of the slices and top with egg salad; top with the remaining bread. Cut each sandwich in half with a serrated knife.

step 3

serve

1. Place a sandwich on each of 4 plates and garnish with a serving of vegetable chips. Serve with the carrot salad or serve it on separate plates.

2. When ready for dessert, scoop lemon sorbet into 4 small dessert bowls and top with blueberries.

Tomato and Avocado Egg-Salad Sandwiches
Single serving is 1/4 of the total recipe
CALORIES 435; PROTEIN 18g; CARBS 44g;
TOTAL FAT 25g; SAT FAT 5g; CHOLESTEROL 329mg;
SODIUM 777mg; FIBER 9g

two-olive muffuletta
tomato juice cocktails
pralines and cream
ice cream

shopping list

Crusty round peasant bread

Pimiento-stuffed green salad olives

Kalamata olives, pitted and sliced

Pepperoncini

Iceberg lettuce

Ripe tomatoes

Ripe avocado, preferably Haas

Low-fat provolone, such as Alpine Lace Provo-Lo, sliced

Lemon

Tomato juice

Celery sticks (from the salad bar)

Pralines and cream ice cream

from your pantry

Fruity olive oil

Red wine vinegar

Freshly ground black pepper

serves 4

beforeyoustart
Chill the tomato juice.

step **1** make the **two-olive muffuletta**

step **2** prepare the **tomato juice cocktails**

step **3** **serve**

luckyforyou
Small quality bread bakeries and gourmet shops have had an enormous effect on the quality of bread-making in general. Now many supermarkets have their own bakery departments that offer a wide variety of artisan-type loaves daily. For muffuletta, you need a good crusty round loaf, be it French, Italian, or even marbled rye. The crust has to be sturdy enough to serve as a container.

"I like the way muffuletta looks almost as much as I like the way it tastes!"

—minutemeals' Chef Miriam

step 1

make the **two-olive muffuletta**

1 crusty round peasant bread

1/2 cup pimiento-stuffed green salad olives

1/2 cup pitted sliced kalamata olives

1/2 cup drained pepperoncini

3 tablespoons fruity olive oil

1 teaspoon red wine vinegar

2 cups shredded iceberg lettuce (1 small head)

2 large ripe tomatoes

1 large ripe avocado, preferably Haas

1/2 pound sliced low-fat provolone

1. With a bread knife, halve the peasant bread horizontally. Remove the top and reserve. From the bottom half, remove most of the crumb inside, leaving about a 1-inch shell.

2. On a cutting board, coarsely chop together the green olives, kalamata olives, and pepperoncini. Transfer the salad to a bowl and add the olive oil and vinegar; toss to combine. Spoon one-quarter of the olive salad into the bottom of the bread shell.

3. Chop enough iceberg lettuce to measure 2 cups. Rinse, pat dry, and thinly slice the tomatoes. Halve, pit, and peel the avocado; chop.

4. Top the olive salad in the bread shell with the lettuce and top the lettuce with an even layer of tomato slices. Arrange the slices of provolone over the tomatoes. Scatter the avocado over the tomatoes.

5. Spoon the remaining olive salad over the avocado and replace the top of the loaf, pressing down on it firmly.

step 2

prepare the **tomato juice cocktails**

1 lemon

1 bottle (32 ounces) chilled tomato juice

Freshly ground black pepper to taste

4 celery sticks

1. Cut the lemon into 4 wedges.

2. Pour the tomato juice into 4 tall glasses and add fresh pepper to taste.

3. Add a celery stick to each glass and garnish each serving with a lemon wedge. Place the glasses on the table.

step 3

serve

1. Place the cutting board with the muffuletta on it on the table. With a large serrated knife, cut it into generous wedges and place them on 4 plates.

2. When ready for dessert, scoop the ice cream into 4 small dessert bowls. Serve.

Two-Olive Muffuletta
Single serving is 1/4 of the total recipe
CALORIES 611; PROTEIN 25g; CARBS 57g;
TOTAL FAT 38g; SAT FAT 12g; CHOLESTEROL 30mg;
SODIUM 1237mg; FIBER 8g

scandinavian tomato and egg sandwiches

potato chips
chilled beet salad
red berries with butter cookies

menu gameplan

serves 4

shopping list

Rustic whole-wheat or rye bread, unsliced

Tomatoes

Peeled hard-cooked eggs (from the salad bar)

Kirby cucumber

Caponata or container of hummus

Ripe olives, pitted (canned or from the deli counter)

Fresh dill or watercress

Quick-thaw frozen strawberries

Quick-thaw frozen raspberries

Danish butter cookies

Pickled beets, sliced

Potato chips

from your pantry

Salt and pepper

beforeyoustart

Place pickled beets in the refrigerator. Thaw the frozen strawberries and raspberries according to the packages.

step **1** assemble the **sandwiches**

step **2** prepare the **red berries with butter cookies**

step **3** plate the **chilled beet salad**

step **4** **serve**

 Hard-cooked eggs that you prepare from your own fresh eggs can be stored up to a week in the refrigerator. Here, however, we've called for hard-cooked eggs from the salad bar of your supermarket. They should be used within a day or so of purchase to ensure safety.

"Along with the hard-cooked eggs, buy sliced cucumbers and sliced tomatoes at the salad bar. Then try the Scandinavian presentation."

—minutemeals' Chef Ruth

step 1

assemble the **scandinavian tomato and egg sandwiches**

1 loaf of rustic whole-wheat or rye bread

4 small or 3 medium tomatoes

Salt and pepper to taste

4 peeled hard-cooked eggs

1 small Kirby cucumber

1 small can (7 1/2 ounces) caponata or container of hummus

8 pitted ripe olives

Sprigs of fresh dill or watercress for garnish

1. Cut the bread into 4 large thick slices. Toast in a toaster oven until lightly colored. Transfer each slice to a serving plate.

2. Cut a thin slice off the top and bottom of each tomato, then thinly slice. Season with salt and pepper. Cut the eggs into quarters lengthwise. Thinly slice the cucumber. Season the eggs and cucumber with salt and pepper.

3. Spread each slice of bread with about 2 tablespoons caponata. Make a cut halfway through each tomato slice. Twist the ends in opposite directions so that the slice will stand up. Arrange about 4 slices of tomato on each toast slice. Add 4 egg quarters, cucumber slices, and 2 ripe olives to each sandwich, arranging the ingredients upright as much as possible. Garnish with sprigs of fresh dill. (For a quicker assembly, slice the ingredients and layer them on the bread, beginning with the tomatoes, then the eggs, cucumbers, and olives.)

step 2

prepare the **red berries with butter cookies**

1/2 bag (12 ounces) quick-thaw frozen strawberries

1/2 bag (12 ounces) quick-thaw frozen raspberries

Danish butter cookies

1. Thaw the berries in the microwave according to the directions on the packages.

2. In a medium bowl, combine the berries, tossing gently to mix.

3. Arrange the butter cookies on a serving plate.

step 3

plate the **chilled beet salad**

1 jar (16 ounces) sliced pickled beets, chilled

Fresh dill (optional) for garnish

Drain the beets and place in a medium serving bowl. Snip fresh dill over the top, if desired. Place the bowl on the table.

step 4

serve

1. If you have arranged the sandwiches Scandinavian style, carefully transfer the plates to the table. Garnish each serving with potato chips at the table. Serve with the beet salad, on separate plates, if desired.

2. When ready for dessert, toss the berries gently. Serve in 4 small bowls with the butter cookies as an accompaniment. Or, crumble the cookies over the berries before serving.

Scandinavian Tomato and Egg Sandwiches
Single serving is 1/4 of the total recipe
CALORIES 354; PROTEIN 15g; CARBS 39g;
TOTAL FAT 15g; SAT FAT 2g; CHOLESTEROL 215mg;
SODIUM 586mg; FIBER 4g

vegetable pan bagnat

apple walnut slaw
marble pound cake with warm chocolate sauce

menu gameplan

shopping list

Walnuts

Crisp apples

Shredded red cabbage
(from the salad bar or from
the produce department)

Shredded green cabbage
(from the salad bar or from
the produce department)

Arugula or watercress

Tomatoes

Jarred roasted red peppers

Crusty French bread

Kalamata olives, pitted

Herb-and-garlic-flavored
goat cheese

Marble pound cake

from your pantry

Vinaigrette dressing,
store-bought or homemade

Salt and pepper

Extra virgin olive oil

Chocolate sauce

serves 4

beforeyoustart

Place the jar of chocolate sauce in a
pan of hot tap water to stand until
serving time.

step **1** prepare the **apple walnut slaw**

step **2** assemble the **vegetable pan bagnat**

step **3** **serve**

headsup

Just as good bread is an essential ingredient for this sandwich, so is flavorful olive oil. Even though you aren't using very much of it, you want an oil with a maximum amount of flavor to imbue the bread and vegetables. Extra virgin olive oil will do that. Virgin olive oil, which is slightly higher in acid but also made from the first pressing, would be our next choice.

"There's a reason for using an ingredient like herb-and-garlic-flavored goat cheese. Being already 'seasoned,' it cuts down on the number of ingredients."

—minutemeals' Chef Paul

step 1

prepare the **apple walnut slaw**

- 1/3 cup walnut pieces
- 2 crisp apples
- 2 cups shredded red cabbage
- 2 cups shredded green cabbage
- 3 tablespoons vinaigrette dressing, store-bought or homemade
- Salt and pepper to taste

1. Spread the walnuts on a paper towel. Microwave on High for 1 minute, or until fragrant. Place in a medium bowl.

2. Cut the apples into quarters and remove the cores. Thinly slice the apples and add them to the bowl with the red and green cabbage and vinaigrette. Season with salt and pepper and toss well.

step 2

assemble the **vegetable pan bagnat**

- 1 bunch arugula or watercress, rinsed and patted dry
- 2 medium tomatoes
- 1 jar (7 ounces) roasted red peppers
- 1 long loaf crusty French bread (about 12 inches)
- 2 tablespoons extra virgin olive oil
- 1/2 cup pitted kalamata olives
- Salt and pepper to taste
- 1 log (4 ounces) herb-and-garlic-flavored goat cheese

1. Rinse the arugula or watercress, remove any tough stems, and spin or pat dry. Rinse, pat dry, and slice the tomatoes. Drain, rinse, and pat dry the roasted peppers; cut them into strips.

2. Cut the bread in half lengthwise. Open the bread so that the cut sides face up. Drizzle or brush with the olive oil. Layer arugula, roasted peppers, olives, and tomatoes on the bottom half of the loaf. Season with salt and pepper.

3. Crumble the goat cheese over the tomatoes, using a fork. Cover with the top half of the loaf and press down to seal.

step 3

serve

1. With a serrated knife, cut the sandwich into 4 pieces and place each on a dinner plate. Serve with the slaw.

2. When ready for dessert, slice the pound cake into generous pieces, place each on a dessert plate, and spoon warm chocolate sauce over the top. Or, transfer the chocolate sauce to a serving bowl and serve it separately to be added at the table.

Vegetable Pan Bagnat
Single serving is 1/4 of the total recipe
CALORIES 350; PROTEIN 13g; CARBS 31g;
TOTAL FAT 21g; SAT FAT 7g; CHOLESTEROL 22mg;
SODIUM 601mg; FIBER 4g

warm pita pockets
with mushroom and zucchini frittata

tomato, feta, and basil salad

chocolate pudding
with pecans

menu
gameplan

shopping list

Zucchini

Presliced button mushrooms
(from the produce department)

Pre-shredded Cheddar or
Swiss cheese

Pita pockets, whole-wheat
or regular

Basil leaves

Vine-ripe tomatoes

Crumbled feta cheese

Chocolate pudding (from the
prepared foods section)

Pecans

Instant whipped cream
(optional)

from your pantry

Butter

Large eggs

Salt and pepper

Dried or fresh chives

Extra virgin olive oil

serves 4

beforeyoustart

Preheat the oven to 350°F to cook the
frittata and heat the pita pockets.

step **1** make the **mushroom and zucchini frittata**

step **2** assemble the **tomato, feta, and basil salad**

step **3** **serve**

headsup

We've made our frittata with button mushrooms, but you can substitute "wild" mushrooms, such as cremini. You will have to allow for some additional prep time to clean the cremini and slice them. Reserve cremini-filled frittata for the grown-ups and serve it not in pita pockets, but on lightly toasted buttered slices of semolina bread.

"You can serve frittata hot or at room temperature, or vary the vegetables, or gratinée it. Frittatas are fabulously accommodating!"

—minutemeals' Chef Ruth

make the **mushroom and zucchini frittata**

2 small zucchini
(3/4 pound total weight)

1 box (8 ounces) presliced button mushrooms

2 tablespoons butter

8 large eggs

Salt and pepper to taste

3 tablespoons dried or fresh snipped chives

1 cup (4 ounces) pre-shredded Cheddar or Swiss cheese

4 large pita pockets, whole-wheat or regular

1. Preheat the oven to 350°F.

2. Trim the ends of the zucchini and coarsely chop. Clean the mushrooms, place in a food processor, and coarsely chop. (You should have about 3 cups.)

3. Melt the butter in a large oven-proof skillet over medium heat. Add the zucchini and mushrooms and cook, stirring occasionally, until the mushrooms are tender and most of the liquid has evaporated, about 5 minutes.

4. Meanwhile, break the eggs into a large bowl and season with salt and pepper. Add the chives. Whisk until well blended.

5. Pour the egg mixture over the vegetables and cook, stirring lightly, until the edges are barely set, about 2 minutes. Sprinkle with the Cheddar or Swiss. Transfer the skillet to the oven and bake for 8 to 10 minutes, until the center of the omelet is just set and most of the cheese is melted.

6. While the frittata bakes, wrap the pita pockets loosely in aluminum foil. Place in the oven alongside the frittata for the last 5 minutes of cooking time to heat through.

step 2

assemble the **tomato, feta, and basil salad**

8 basil leaves

4 large vine-ripe tomatoes

1/4 cup crumbled feta cheese, plain or flavored

Salt and pepper to taste

2 to 3 tablespoons extra virgin olive oil

Rinse the basil leaves and tomatoes and pat dry. Cut the tomatoes into thin slices and arrange in circles on a serving plate. Scatter the crumbled feta over them and season with salt and pepper. Drizzle the olive oil over all, then tear the basil leaves into pieces and scatter over the salad. Place the plate on the table.

step 3

serve

1. Remove the pita pockets and frittata from the oven. Cut the pita pockets in half. Cut the frittata into 8 wedges and with a broad spatula, tuck a wedge into each of the pockets. Place on a serving platter or individual serving plates. Serve, with the tomato salad alongside.

2. When ready for dessert, spoon chocolate pudding into 4 small dessert bowls and sprinkle with pecans. Serve, with whipped cream, if desired.

Warm Pita Pockets with Mushroom and Zucchini Frittata
Single serving is 1/4 of the total recipe
CALORIES 341; PROTEIN 27g; CARBS 37g;
TOTAL FAT 10g; SAT FAT 0g; CHOLESTEROL 30mg;
SODIUM 674mg; FIBER 2g

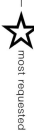

☆ beany wraps

tomato and swiss cheese salad

summer fruit bowl of plums, grapes, and cherries

blondies

menu
gameplan

serves 4

beforeyoustart

Place the fruits for dessert in a bowl and chill until serving time.

step 1 assemble the **tomato and swiss cheese salad**

step 2 make the **beany wraps**

step 3 **serve**

shopping list

Ripe tomatoes

Swiss cheese, sliced

Garbanzo beans (chickpeas)

Scallions

Fresh parsley

Flour tortillas
(8- to 9-inch diameter)

Fresh fruit, such as seedless grapes, plums, and cherries

Blondies

from the salad bar

Baby spinach leaves

Celery stalk

from your pantry

Salad dressing of choice, store-bought or homemade

Reduced-fat or light mayonnaise

Sweet pickle relish

Dijon mustard

Salt and pepper

luckyforyou We've called for plain flour
tortillas for these wraps, but
if you look in the deli area of your supermarket you will
probably happen upon a selection of differently flavored
wraps, including tomato, spinach, and whole wheat. You
can also use lavash.

"Some people don't want to use the food processor because they can't stand washing it. But a processor chops the beans here in seconds."

step 1

assemble the **tomato and swiss cheese salad**

3 ripe medium tomatoes

Baby spinach leaves for lining the platter

8 ounces sliced Swiss cheese

2 to 3 tablespoons salad dressing of choice

1. Rinse, pat dry, and thinly slice the tomatoes.

2. Line a serving platter with the spinach leaves. Arrange the tomato and cheese slices, alternating them, on the spinach. Drizzle the salad with a dressing of choice. Place the platter on the table.

step 2

make the **beany wraps**

1 can (19 ounces) garbanzo beans (chickpeas)

3 scallions

1 celery stalk

3 tablespoons reduced-fat or light mayonnaise

2 tablespoons sweet pickle relish

2 tablespoons chopped fresh parsley

1 tablespoon Dijon mustard

Salt and pepper to taste

4 flour tortillas (8- to 9-inch diameter)

1. Drain and rinse the garbanzo beans. Place in a food processor and pulse briefly, just until broken into small chunks. (The beans should not be processed until smooth.) Or, place the beans on a chopping surface and roughly chop. Place the chopped beans in a medium bowl.

2. Trim the scallions to about 4 inches in length; finely chop. Chop the celery. Add the scallions, celery, mayonnaise, relish, parsley, and mustard to the beans, mixing lightly with a fork. Season with salt and pepper. Chill for 5 to 10 minutes.

3. If desired, gently warm the tortillas: Place between sheets of just-damp paper towels and heat in the microwave just until warm. (Do not overheat the tortillas. They should not be too crisp.)

step 3

serve

1. Place a tortilla on each serving plate. Divide the filling equally among the tortillas and spread it almost to the edges. Fold in the edges on opposite sides and roll up each tortilla to form a wrap. Serve, with the tomato and Swiss cheese salad.

2. When ready for dessert, bring the fruit bowl and the blondies to the table with dessert plates or bowls, or just napkins.

Beany Wraps
Single serving is ¼ of the total recipe
CALORIES 283; PROTEIN 9g; CARBS 48g;
TOTAL FAT 6g; SAT FAT 0g; CHOLESTEROL 0mg;
SODIUM 610mg; FIBER 0g

pepper and eggplant wraps

black bean salad

dulce de leche frozen yogurt sundaes

menu gameplan

serves 4

step 1 prepare the **pepper and eggplant wraps**

step 2 assemble the **black bean salad**

3 prepare the **dulce de leche frozen yogurt sundaes**

4 **serve**

shopping list

Red pepper

Green pepper

Thin Japanese eggplants or eggplant

Zucchini

Goat cheese or crumbled feta

Flour tortillas (9- to 10-inch diameter)

Olive tapenade or green or ripe olive paste

Black beans

Tomato

Chopped scallions (from the salad bar)

Greek-style vinaigrette dresing

Prewashed mixed salad greens

Caramel sauce

Dulce de leche frozen yogurt

Cashew pieces

from your pantry

Olive oil

Pre-chopped garlic

Salt and pepper

headsup Some olive tapenade includes a trace of anchovies. If, as a vegetarian, you do not eat fish, substitute mushroom tapenade.

"Sometimes a wrap is really what you want for a light dinner or easy lunch. The filling here is especially flavorful."

—minutemeals' Chef Ruth

prepare the **pepper and eggplant wraps**

1 medium red pepper

1 medium green pepper

2 small thin Japanese eggplants or 1 medium eggplant

2 small zucchini (about 1/2 pound)

3 tablespoons olive oil

2 teaspoons pre-chopped garlic

Salt and pepper to taste

3 ounces goat cheese or crumbled feta

4 flour tortillas (9- to 10-inch diameter)

1/4 cup olive tapenade or green or ripe olive paste

1. Core and seed the red and green peppers; cut into strips. Cut the Japanese eggplants into 1/4-inch-thick slices. If using larger eggplant, quarter it lengthwise. Stack the slices and cut into 1/4 inch thick strips. Trim the ends of the zucchini and cut into thin slices.

2. Heat the olive oil in a large deep nonstick skillet over medium-high heat. Add the garlic and cook, stirring, until lightly colored. Add the eggplant, zucchini, and pepper strips. Stir-fry for 8 to 10 minutes, or until the vegetables are tender. Season with salt and pepper. Sprinkle with the goat cheese or feta.

3. Meanwhile, heat the tortillas: Place the tortillas between sheets of just-damp paper towels and heat in the microwave just until warm. (Do not overheat as the tortillas should not be too crisp.)

assemble the **black bean salad**

1 can (15 to 16 ounces) black beans

1 large tomato

1/2 cup chopped scallions

2 to 3 tablespoons store-bought Greek-style vinaigrette dressing

Salt and pepper to taste

2 cups prewashed colorful mixed salad greens

1. Rinse and drain the beans. Rinse the tomato, pat dry, and chop.

2. In a medium bowl, combine the beans, tomato, scallions, dressing, and salt and pepper. Toss to coat.

3. Place the greens in a shallow serving bowl and mound the bean salad on top. Place the bowl on the table.

prepare the **dulce de leche frozen yogurt sundaes**

1 small jar caramel sauce

1 pint dulce de leche frozen yogurt

1/2 cup cashew pieces

Place the jar of caramel sauce in a small saucepan of hot water or in a covered microwave safe dish and microwave until pourable.

serve

1. Place a warm tortilla on each serving plate. Spread each with about 1 tablespoon tapenade. Spoon some of the hot vegetable mixture onto the tortilla. Fold in the edges on opposite sides and roll up to form a wrap. Make wraps with the remaining tortillas and filling in the same manner. Serve.

2. When ready for dessert, scoop the frozen yogurt into 4 small dessert bowls. Top with warm caramel sauce and garnish with chopped cashews. Serve, with additional caramel sauce, if desired.

Pepper and Eggplant Wraps
Single serving is 1/4 of the total recipe
CALORIES 466; PROTEIN 13g; CARBS 55g; TOTAL FAT 23g; SAT FAT 4g; CHOLESTEROL 10mg; SODIUM 467mg; FIBER 8g

vegetable mu shu wraps

sesame carrot salad

vanilla ice cream
with candied ginger

menu
gameplan

shopping list

Lime (for juice)

Spring roll wrappers or flour
tortillas (6- to 8-inch diameter)

Presliced mushrooms
(from the produce department)

Pre-shredded cabbage
(bagged, from the produce
department)

Stir-fry sauce

Hoisin sauce

Candied ginger

Vanilla ice cream

from the salad bar

Chopped scallions

Shredded carrots (or from the
produce department)

from your pantry

Peanut or vegetable oil

Toasted sesame oil

Large eggs

headsup Many supermarkets now have
a well-stocked specialty Asian
foods section, where you can do a lot of the shopping for
this menu. Here's what you should be looking for if you
don't already have them on hand: Toasted sesame oil,
stir-fry sauce, hoisin sauce. You may also find stir-fry
sauce in the produce department among the refrigerated
bottled items. Once opened, the oil and sauces should
be stored in the refrigerator.

serves 4

beforeyoustart

Preheat the oven to 350°F. Remove the
ice cream from the freezer.

step **1** assemble the **salad**

step **2** prepare the **warm wrappers**

step **3** make the **vegetable mu shu wraps**

step **4** prepare the **ice cream**

step **5** **serve**

"The whole family will love making these wraps. They're fun. Try them with tortillas or ready-made crepes, too."

—minutemeals' Chef Paul

step 1

assemble the **sesame carrot salad**

2 tablespoons peanut or vegetable oil

1 tablespoon lime juice (1 lime)

2 teaspoons toasted sesame oil

8 ounces shredded carrots

1/4 cup chopped scallions

Whisk together the peanut oil, lime juice, and sesame oil in a medium bowl. Add the carrots and scallions, and toss to combine. Place the bowl on the table.

step 2

prepare the **warm wrappers**

8 spring roll wrappers or flour tortillas (6- to 8-inch diameter)

1. Preheat the oven to 350°F.

2. Stack the tortillas and wrap the stack loosely in aluminum foil. Place in the oven to heat while you make the mu shu filling.

step 3

make the **vegetable mu shu wraps**

4 large eggs

1 1/2 tablespoons peanut or vegetable oil

1 box (8 ounces) presliced mushrooms

1 bag (16 ounces) pre-shredded cabbage

1 cup chopped scallions

1/4 cup jarred stir-fry sauce

1/4 cup hoisin sauce for serving

1. Beat the eggs in a small bowl.

2. Heat 1/2 tablespoon of the peanut oil in a large nonstick skillet over medium heat. Pour in the eggs and cook, shaking the pan and lifting the edges to allow the uncooked egg to flow underneath, for 2 minutes, or until the eggs are almost set. Cut the egg sheet (or pancake) in half with a spatula and flip each half; cook 1 minute. Turn out onto a cutting board. Cut the egg sheets crosswise into 1/4-inch strips.

3. Add the remaining 1 tablespoon oil to the skillet. Increase the heat to high, add the mushrooms, and cook for 4 minutes without stirring, until just tender. Add the cabbage and scallions and cook for 7 minutes, tossing occasionally with 2 spoons, or until just tender-crisp.

4. Stir in the stir-fry sauce and cook for 1 minute. Add the egg strips and cook, tossing to coat. Remove the pan from the heat.

step 4

prepare the **vanilla ice cream with candied ginger**

2 tablespoons candied ginger, or to taste

1 pint vanilla ice cream

1. With a sharp knife, chop the ginger into bite-size pieces.

2. Scoop the ice cream into a serving bowl. Add the chopped ginger and with a rubber spatula, swirl the pieces into the ice cream, distributing them evenly. Place the bowl in the freezer until serving time.

step 5

serve

1. Bring the filling, hoisin sauce, and wrappers to the table. Have each person spread a little of the hoisin in the center of the wrapper, spoon filling on top, and roll up envelope-style. Serve with the carrot salad.

2. When ready for dessert, scoop the ice cream into small dessert bowls and serve, with additional candied ginger on the side, if desired.

Vegetable Mu Shu Wraps
Single serving is 1/4 of the total recipe
(7-inch flour tortillas used for analysis)

CALORIES 349; PROTEIN 13g; CARBS 44g;
TOTAL FAT 14g; SAT FAT 2g; CHOLESTEROL 217mg;
SODIUM 705mg; FIBER 2g

☆ salad pizza
roasted bananas with frozen yogurt

menu gameplan

shopping list

Prebaked pizza crust
(12 inches in diameter
and weighing 16 ounces)

White beans

Prewashed spring or
baby salad greens

Cherry tomatoes
(from the salad bar)

Jarred roasted peppers

Capers

Pre-shredded light (or lite)
mozzarella

Firm-but-ripe bananas

Low-fat vanilla frozen yogurt

from your pantry

Extra virgin olive oil

Balsamic vinegar

Dijon mustard

Salt and pepper

Vegetable cooking spray

serves 4

beforeyoustart
Preheat the oven to 450°F to bake
the pizza.

step 1   make the **salad pizza**

step 2   prepare the **roasted bananas with frozen yogurt**

step 3   **serve**

headsup
Don't confuse light mozzarella
(also spelled "lite" by some
manufacturers) with part-skim mozzarella. Part-skim is
somewhat higher in both fat and calories. You want light
(or lite) mozzarella here. Look for it in resealable bags in
the cheese section of the dairy case in your supermarket.

"You really feel satisfied after eating salad pizza. I love it. There's a wonderful amount of topping, a lot to sink your teeth into."

—minutemeals' Chef Marge

make the **salad pizza**

A prebaked pizza crust
(12 inches in diameter
and weighing 16 ounces)

1 can (15 ounces) white beans

8 cups prewashed spring or
baby salad greens

1 cup cherry tomatoes
(about 8 large)

1 jar (7 ounces) roasted
peppers

2 tablespoons drained capers

2 tablespoons extra virgin
olive oil

1 tablespoon balsamic vinegar

$1/2$ teaspoon Dijon mustard

Salt and pepper to taste

$1/2$ cup pre-shredded light
(or lite) mozzarella

1. Preheat the oven to 450°F. Place the pizza crust on a large baking sheet.

2. While the oven heats, prepare the topping: Drain and rinse the white beans. Cut the salad greens into 1-inch pieces. Lightly mash about half the beans with the back of a fork. In a bowl, toss the greens and beans together.

3. Rinse the cherry tomatoes, pat dry, and cut into quarters. Drain the roasted peppers and cut them into $1/2$-inch pieces. Add the peppers, tomatoes, capers, and remaining beans to the salad mixture.

4. In a small bowl, combine the olive oil, vinegar, mustard, and salt and pepper. Add the dressing to the salad mixture and toss to combine.

5. Top the pizza crust with the salad mixture, then scatter the grated mozzarella over the top. Bake the pizza for 10 minutes. Do not turn the oven off after baking the pizza.

step 2

prepare the **roasted bananas with frozen yogurt**

Vegetable cooking spray

2 large firm-but-ripe bananas

Low-fat vanilla frozen yogurt,
softened

1. Spray a large baking sheet with sides lightly with vegetable cooking spray.

2. Peel the bananas, then halve them crosswise and lengthwise to make 8 spears. Arrange in a single layer on the baking sheet. Roast for 5 to 7 minutes, or until lightly colored and hot.

3. Remove the yogurt from the freezer to soften slightly.

step 3

serve

1. With a pizza cutter or sharp knife, cut the pizza into wedges and serve at once. (Forks and knives are recommended.)

2. When ready for dessert, divide the bananas while they are still hot among 4 dessert plates and top each serving with frozen yogurt. Serve.

Salad Pizza
Single serving is $1/4$ of the total recipe
CALORIES 433; PROTEIN 21g; CARBS 62g;
TOTAL FAT 14g; SAT FAT 2g; CHOLESTEROL 7mg;
SODIUM 565mg; FIBER 14g

☆ mexican pizza

avocado salad

pink grapefruit with cinnamon thins

menu
gameplan

shopping list

Prebaked thin pizza crust
(10 ounces)

Fat-free vegetarian refried
black beans

Chopped scallions
(from the salad bar)

Pre-shredded Cheddar cheese
or Mexican mix cheese

Iceberg lettuce

Ripe tomato

Salsa, mild or spicy

Ripe avocados, preferably
Haas

Lime (for juice)

Jarred pink grapefruit,
refrigerated (from the
produce department)

Thin cookies

from your pantry

Fruity olive oil

Salt and pepper

Ground cinnamon

serves 4

beforeyoustart

Preheat the oven to 450°F to bake
the pizza.

step 1 make the **mexican pizza**

step 2 prepare the **avocado salad**

step 3 prepare the **pink grapefruit with cinnamon thins**

step 4 **serve**

headsup There can be a sizable differ-
ence among brands in the
amount of sodium per serving for canned refried beans.
We have called for fat-free vegetarian refried black beans
for this pizza and suggest that you do some comparison
shopping before you purchase them. Look for them in
the vegetarian foods section of supermarkets and health
food stores.

"You know, after eating some pizza, you really feel weighed down. Not with this one. It's light. And it's pretty."

—minutemeals' Chef Nancy

step 1

make the **mexican pizza**

- 1 prebaked thin pizza crust (10 ounces)
- 1 can (16 ounces) fat-free vegetarian refried black beans
- 1/2 cup chopped scallions
- 3/4 cup pre-shredded Cheddar cheese or Mexican mix cheese
- 1 cup shredded iceberg lettuce (1 small head)
- 1 cup chopped ripe tomato (1 medium-large)
- 1/4 cup mild or spicy salsa for serving

1. Preheat the oven to 450°F.

2. Place the pizza crust on a large cookie sheet. Spread the crust with the refried beans. Sprinkle with the scallions and top with the cheese. Bake the pizza until the crust is crisp and the cheese is melted, about 10 minutes.

3. While the pizza is baking, chop enough lettuce and tomato to measure 1 cup each. Remove the pizza from the oven and sprinkle with the lettuce and tomato.

step 2

prepare the **avocado salad**

- 2 ripe avocados, preferably Haas
- 1 tablespoon fruity olive oil
- 1 large lime
- Salt and pepper to taste

1. Halve each avocado and remove the pit, but leave the skin on. Put 1 avocado half in each of 4 bowls. Spoon some of the olive oil into the center of each avocado half.

2. Cut the lime in half and squeeze some juice over each avocado half. Season with salt and pepper. Place the bowls on the table for serving.

step 3

prepare the **pink grapefruit with cinnamon thins**

- 1 jar (26 ounces) pink grapefruit in its own juice
- Thin cookies
- Ground cinnamon (optional) for serving

1. Spoon the grapefruit segments, with juice, into 4 dessert bowls and chill until serving time.

2. Plate the cookies.

step 4

serve

1. Remove the pizza to a cutting board. With a pizza cutter or a large sharp knife, cut it into wedges. Divide the wedges among 4 dinner plates. Serve with the salsa and the avocado salad.

2. When ready for dessert, serve the grapefruit with the cinnamon thins. Pass around cinnamon at the table for sprinkling over the grapefruit, if desired.

Mexican Pizza
Single serving is 1/4 of the total recipe
CALORIES 373; PROTEIN 19g; CARBS 48g; TOTAL FAT 13g; SAT FAT 5g; CHOLESTEROL 25mg; SODIUM 933mg; FIBER 5g

phyllo pizza
with broccoli and mozzarella

white bean salad with carrots

fresh pears with golden raisins

menu
gameplan

shopping list

Frozen broccoli florets

Phyllo dough

Canned diced tomatoes

Pre-shredded part-skim mozzarella

White beans

Fresh parsley

Shredded carrots
(from the salad bar or from the produce department)

Roasted garlic salad dressing

Ripe pears

Golden raisins

from your pantry

Olive oil

Dried oregano

Salt and pepper

serves 2

beforeyoustart

Preheat the oven to 450°F. Remove the phyllo from the packaging. Cover with plastic wrap, then with a damp towel.

step 1 make the **phyllo pizza with broccoli and mozzarella**

step 2 assemble the **white bean salad with carrots**

step 3 prepare the **fresh pears with golden raisins**

step 4 **serve**

heads up

Most likely, you will be buying frozen phyllo dough, which means that you will have to anticipate thawing it overnight in the refrigerator. Then, when you start to work with the dough, be sure to cover it to prevent it from drying out.

"Not only does this pizza taste great, it's also a good way to sneak vegetables into your family's diet." —minutemeals' Chef Nancy

step 1

make the **phyllo pizza with broccoli and mozzarella**

1 cup frozen broccoli florets

3 1/2 tablespoons olive oil

8 sheets phyllo dough, about 1/3 pound

1 can (14 1/2 ounces) diced tomatoes

1 teaspoon dried oregano

1 1/2 cups pre-shredded part-skim mozzarella

1. Position the oven rack in the bottom third of the oven. Preheat the oven to 450 °F.

2. Put the frozen broccoli florets in a microwave-safe dish. Microwave on High for 1 minute, until thawed.

3. Brush a 12-inch pizza pan with a little of the olive oil. Lay 1 sheet of phyllo in the pan and brush lightly with oil. Lay another sheet crosswise on it, and brush lightly with oil. Lay 2 more sheets on top of these in a slightly rotated crosswise fashion, oiling each sheet lightly. When done, the pan should be evenly covered with the 4 phyllo sheets.

4. Lay a sheet of phyllo on your work surface, oil half of it, and fold it over across its shortest width. Lay this folded sheet on top of and in the middle of the 4 stacked sheets. Oil it lightly. Oil and fold the remaining 3 phyllo sheets in the same manner, rotating them as you lay them on top of each other so that they cover the bottom sheets evenly.

5. Roll up the edges of the dough to form a round pizza crust. Brush the crust with the remaining olive oil.

6. Drain the diced tomatoes; scatter them over the crust. Sprinkle with the oregano, add the broccoli, and finish with the mozzarella. Bake until the crust is a deep golden and the cheese is speckled with brown, about 10 minutes.

step 2

assemble the **white bean salad with carrots**

1 can white beans (15 to 16 ounces)

2 tablespoons chopped fresh parsley

1/2 cup shredded carrots

2 to 3 tablespoons roasted garlic salad dressing

Salt and pepper to taste

1. Rinse and drain the beans. Chop enough parsley to measure 2 tablespoons.

2. In a medium bowl, combine the beans, carrots, parsley, and dressing. Season with salt and pepper and toss to combine. Place the bowl and 2 salad plates on the table.

step 3

prepare the **fresh pears with golden raisins**

4 ripe pears

Golden raisins

Rinse each pear, pat dry and place in a dessert bowl. Place the raisins in a small bowl.

step 4

serve

1. Remove the pizza to a cutting board. With a pizza cutter or a large sharp knife cut it into wedges. Divide the wedges between 2 dinner plates and serve.

2. When ready for dessert, serve the pears with the raisins.

Phyllo Pizza with Broccoli and Mozzarella
Single serving is 1/2 of the total recipe

CALORIES 766; PROTEIN 35g; CARBS 54g; TOTAL FAT 46g; SAT FAT 15g; CHOLESTEROL 53mg; SODIUM 1917mg; FIBER 3g

phyllo pizza
with ricotta and pesto

spinach salad with red pepper

lemon ice

serves 2

shopping list

Phyllo dough

Light ricotta cheese

Prepared pesto

Tomato

Slivered almonds

Lemon ice

from the salad bar

Baby spinach leaves

Thin red pepper slices

from your pantry

Olive oil

Dried red pepper flakes (optional)

Garlic salt (optional)

Grated Parmesan cheese (optional)

Vinaigrette dressing, store-bought or homemade

Salt and pepper

beforeyoustart

Preheat the oven to 450°F. Remove the phyllo from the packaging. Cover with plastic wrap, then with a damp towel.

step **1** make the **phyllo pizza with ricotta and pesto**

step **2** assemble the **spinach salad with red pepper**

step **3** **serve**

headsup If you have made the pizza menu that immediately pre-cedes this one on page 31, you know to treat phyllo dough with due respect. Note the pointers on page 30 before working with it.

make the **phyllo pizza with ricotta and pesto**

3 tablespoons olive oil

8 sheets phyllo dough, about 1/3 pound

8 ounces light ricotta cheese

2 tablespoons prepared pesto

1 large tomato

Dried red pepper flakes for serving (optional)

Garlic salt for serving (optional)

Grated Parmesan cheese for serving (optional)

1. Preheat the oven to 450°.

2. Brush a 12-inch pizza pan with a little of the olive oil. Lay 1 sheet of phyllo in the pan and brush lightly with oil. Lay another sheet crosswise on top of it, and brush lightly with oil. Lay 2 more sheets on top of these in a slightly rotated crosswise fashion, oiling each sheet lightly. When done, the pan should be evenly covered with the 4 phyllo sheets.

3. Lay a sheet of phyllo on the work surface. Oil half of it and fold it over across its shortest width. Lay this folded sheet on top of and in the middle of the 4 stacked sheets. Oil it lightly. Oil and fold the 3 remaining phyllo sheets in the same manner, rotating them as you lay them on top of each other so that they cover the bottom sheets evenly.

4. Roll up the edges of the dough to form a round pizza crust with a 12-inch diameter. Brush the phyllo with the remaining olive oil.

5. Stir the ricotta and pesto together but not too vigorously. (There should be streaks.) Spread over the crust.

6. Slice the tomato into thin rounds and place on the ricotta. Bake the pizza until golden, about 10 minutes.

assemble the **spinach salad with red pepper**

4 loosely packed cups baby spinach leaves

1 cup thin red pepper slices

2 tablespoons vinaigrette dressing

Salt and pepper to taste

2 tablespoons slivered almonds

In a medium salad bowl, combine the spinach, pepper strips, and vinaigrette. Add salt and pepper and toss. Sprinkle the almonds over the top. Place the bowl on the table.

serve

1. Remove the pizza to a cutting board. With a pizza cutter or large sharp knife, cut it into 6 wedges. Divide the wedges between 2 dinner plates and serve, if desired, with the pepper flakes, garlic salt, or Parmesan at the table.

2. When ready for dessert, scoop the ice into 2 small dessert bowls. Serve.

Phyllo Pizza with Ricotta and Pesto
Single serving is 1/2 of the total recipe
CALORIES 663; PROTEIN 22g; CARBS 51g; TOTAL FAT 41g; SAT FAT 5g; CHOLESTEROL 33mg; SODIUM 613mg; FIBER 2g

minute

chapter 2

soup and stew menus

cool avocado soup
with salsa

spring greens vinaigrette with radishes

cheese straws

raspberries and florentine cookies

shopping list

Ripe avocados, preferably Haas

Plain lowfat yogurt

Lemon (for juice)

Salsa

Arugula (optional)

Radishes

Cannellini beans

Prewashed spring or baby greens

Cheese straws (packaged)

Fresh or quick-thaw frozen raspberries

Florentine cookies (from bakery)

from your pantry

Vegetable broth

Tabasco sauce

Salt and fresh pepper

Ice

Red wine vinaigrette dressing, store-bought

Orange juice

serves 4

beforeyoustart

Place the soup bowls and salad plates in the refrigerator to chill.

step 1 make the **cool avocado soup with salsa**

step 2 assemble the **spring greens vinaigrette with radishes**

step 3 prepare the **raspberries and florentine cookies**

step 4 serve

luckyforyou

Even though the arugula in the soup is optional, it adds lovely color and texture to the soup. Sprigs of parsley or the tender tops of watercress sprigs can also be used.

"Some people are devoted to their blenders, and you can make this soup in a blender, but you will have to do it in batches."

—minutemeals' Chef Ruth

step 1

make the **cool avocado soup with salsa**

2 ripe medium avocados, preferably Haas

1 small container (8 ounces) plain lowfat yogurt

1 tablespoon fresh lemon juice (1/2 lemon)

3 cups vegetable broth, preferably chilled

Dash of Tabasco sauce

Salt to taste

10 ice cubes

1 cup salsa for serving

1 cup chopped arugula for serving (optional)

1. Cut the avocados in half and remove the pits. With a spoon, scoop the avocado out of the shells and into a food processor. Add the yogurt and lemon juice. Process until the avocado is almost completely mashed. Through the feed tube, gradually add 1 cup of the broth, processing until smooth. Season with Tabasco sauce and salt.

2. Add the ice cubes and process until the ice is almost completely melted. Transfer to a bowl and stir in the remaining 2 cups broth. Refrigerate while you prepare the rest of the meal.

3. If using arugula, rinse, spin dry, and chop enough to measure 1 cup.

step 2

assemble the **spring greens vinaigrette with radishes**

1 small bunch of radishes

1 can (15 ounces) cannellini beans

1 bag (5 ounces) prewashed spring or baby greens

1/4 cup store-bought red wine vinaigrette dressing

Freshly ground black pepper to taste

1. Clean the radishes and slice thinly. Rinse and drain the beans.

2. Divide the greens among 4 salad plates and top with radishes and some of the beans.

step 3

prepare the **raspberries and florentine cookies**

2 half-pint baskets fresh raspberries or 1 bag (12 ounces) quick-thaw frozen raspberries

4 tablespoons orange juice, or more to taste

Florentine cookies

Rinse the fresh berries in a colander. If using frozen berries, thaw them in the microwave according to the directions on the package. Divide the berries among 4 dessert bowls and chill until serving time.

step 4

serve

1. Stir the soup. With a slotted spoon, remove any pieces of unmelted ice. Ladle the soup into the chilled bowls and garnish each with up to 4 tablespoons each of salsa and arugula, if using. Serve the remaining garnishes in separate bowls on the side.

2. Drizzle each salad with the vinaigrette, season with fresh pepper to taste, and place the plates on the table.

3. Serve the cheese straws in a basket or tall narrow glass with the soup and salad.

4. When ready for dessert, sprinkle each serving of berries with 1 tablespoon orange juice. Serve with the Florentine cookies.

Cool Avocado Soup with Salsa
Single serving is 1/4 of the total recipe
CALORIES 335; PROTEIN 7g; CARBS 30g;
TOTAL FAT 23g; SAT FAT 4g; CHOLESTEROL 12mg;
SODIUM 703mg; FIBER 5g

white gazpacho
carrot and raisin salad
blue cheese and crackers
angel food cake with chocolate sauce and strawberries

menu
gameplan

serves 4

beforeyoustart

Prepare a pitcher of ice water and refrigerate. Chill 4 soup bowls.

step	1	assemble the **carrot and raisin salad**
step	2	plate the **blue cheese and crackers**
step	3	prepare the **angel food cake**
step	4	make the **white gazpacho**
step	5	**serve**

shopping list

Golden raisins

Dried cranberries

Danish blue, Gorgonzola, or domestic blue cheese

Crackers

Quick-thaw frozen strawberries

Angel food cake

Seedless English cucumber

Day-old French bread

Blanched almonds

from the salad bar

Shredded carrots (or from the produce department)

Seedless green grapes

from your pantry

Low-fat or regular mayonnaise

Red wine vinegar

Salt and pepper

Chocolate sauce

Garlic

Fruity olive oil

Don't underestimate the amount of time saved in the simple purchase of a 20-ounce bag of pre-shredded carrots for the salad. It is worth it, and then some: You save not only on prep but also on cleanup.

"If you want to make the gazpacho more luscious, stir in 3 tablespoons of extra virgin olive oil or sour cream right before serving."

—minutemeals' Chef Nancy

assemble the **carrot and raisin salad**

20 ounces shredded carrots

1/2 cup golden raisins

1/2 cup dried cranberries

1/3 cup low-fat or regular mayonnaise

2 tablespoons red wine vinegar

Salt and pepper to taste

Put the carrots, raisins, cranberries, mayonnaise, and vinegar in a salad bowl. Season with salt and pepper and toss to combine. Place the bowl on the table with 4 salad plates.

step 2

plate the **blue cheese and crackers**

A wedge of Danish blue, Gorgonzola, or domestic blue cheese

Assorted crackers

Place the cheese on a serving platter and surround with the crackers. Place the platter on the table.

step 3

prepare the **angel food cake with chocolate sauce and strawberries**

1 bag (12 ounces) quick-thaw frozen strawberries

1 store-bought angel food cake

1 small jar chocolate sauce

Thaw the strawberries in the microwave oven according to the directions on the package.

step 4

make the **white gazpacho**

1 medium seedless English cucumber

1/2 pound seedless green grapes

1 garlic clove

1/2 day-old French bread or 3 to 4 slices other rustic bread

1/3 cup blanched almonds

2 cups ice water, plus more, if desired

3 tablespoons fruity olive oil

2 tablespoons red wine vinegar, plus more, if desired

Salt to taste

1. Peel the cucumber and thinly slice. (You will need 3 cups sliced.) Rinse the grapes; stem enough to measure 1 cup. Peel the garlic.

2. Cut the crusts from the bread. Tear the bread into pieces to measure 1 cup. Put the bread crumbs in a blender or food processor with the garlic and almonds. Grind until the almonds are finely chopped. Add the cucumber slices and grapes and process until very finely chopped.

3. Transfer the mixture to a serving bowl. Stir in 2 cups ice water, the olive oil, vinegar, and salt to taste. Add a small amount of additional ice water to adjust the consistency and more vinegar as desired. Set the bowl on the table with a ladle.

step 5

serve

1. Ladle the soup into the 4 chilled bowls and serve, with the salad and cheese and crackers.

2. When ready for dessert, slice the angel food cake into 4 pieces, drizzle each serving with chocolate sauce, and top with strawberries, and serve. Or serve the sauce and berries separately, to be added at the table by each diner.

White Gazpacho
Single serving is 1/4 of the total recipe
CALORIES 243; PROTEIN 5g; CARBS 19g; TOTAL FAT 18g; SAT FAT 2g; CHOLESTEROL 0mg; SODIUM 126mg; FIBER 3g

jamaican black bean and vegetable soup
spinach and grapefruit salad
warm sesame seed rolls
pecan shortbread sundaes

menu
gameplan

shopping list

Carrots

Green pepper

Black beans

Diced tomatoes with
mild green chiles

Light sour cream

Sliced almonds

Grapefruit sections
(jarred, from the produce
department)

Baby spinach

Ruby grapefruit
salad dressing

Sesame seed rolls

Coffee caramel ice cream

Caramel sauce

Pecan shortbread cookies

from your pantry

Olive oil

Vegetable broth

Ground allspice

Mild cayenne pepper sauce,
such as Frank's Redhot
Sauce

serves 4

beforeyoustart

Transfer the ice cream from the freezer
to the refrigerator to soften slightly.

step **1** make the **jamaican black bean and vegetable soup**

step **2** assemble the **spinach and grapefruit salad**

step **3** prepare the **warm sesame seed rolls**

step **4** prepare the **pecan shortbread sundaes**

step **5** **serve**

headsup
Using the bagged baby
spinach will save you lots of
prep time, as it is already clean. If you purchase bags
of large-leafed spinach that hasn't been triple-washed or
isn't labeled "ready to eat," be certain to rinse it thoroughly
in cold water and dry it well in a salad spinner.

"You can add more flavor to the almonds in the salad by toasting them."

—minutemeals' Chef Paul

step 1

make the **jamaican black bean and vegetable soup**

3 large carrots

1 green pepper

1 can (19 ounces) black beans

1 tablespoon olive oil

1 can (14¹/₂ ounces) vegetable broth

1 can (14¹/₂ ounces) diced tomatoes with mild green chiles

¹/₄ teaspoon ground allspice, or more to taste

1 tablespoon mild cayenne pepper sauce, such as Frank's Redhot Sauce

¹/₃ cup light sour cream for serving

1. Peel and slice the carrots. Coarsely chop the green pepper. Drain but do not rinse the black beans.

2. In a large heavy saucepan, heat the olive oil over medium heat until hot. Add the carrots and green pepper and cook, stirring often, for 4 minutes, until nearly tender.

3. Increase the heat to high. Stir in the beans, broth, tomatoes, and allspice. Bring to a boil, covered. Reduce the heat to medium and simmer for 8 minutes, or until the vegetables are tender. Keep the soup warm, covered.

step 2

assemble the **spinach and grapefruit salad**

2 tablespoons sliced almonds, toasted (optional)

1 cup jarred grapefruit sections

1 bag (5 ounces) baby spinach

¹/₃ cup ruby grapefruit salad dressing

1. Toast the almonds in the microwave, if desired. Drain the grapefruit sections.

2. Place the spinach and grapefruit in large salad bowl and toss gently.

step 3

prepare the **warm sesame seed rolls**

4 sesame seed rolls

Heat the rolls in a toaster oven at 350°F for 5 to 8 minutes. Place in a basket and cover to keep warm. Place the basket on the table.

step 4

prepare the **pecan shortbread sundaes**

1 pint coffee caramel ice cream

¹/₂ cup jarred caramel sauce

12 pecan shortbread cookies

1. Scoop the ice cream into 4 dessert bowls and place in freezer.

2. Heat the caramel sauce in a microwave oven on Medium for 30 to 60 seconds, stirring half way through the cooking time. Keep warm.

3. Put the cookies in a zip-top plastic bag and seal the bag. Crush the cookies with a rolling pin, rolling over the bag several times.

step 5

serve

1. Stir the pepper sauce into the soup. Ladle the soup into 4 soup bowls and serve with the sour cream and additional pepper sauce on the side.

2. Add the dressing to the salad and toss. Divide the salad among 4 salad plates, sprinkle each with some of the almonds, and place the plates on the table.

3. When ready for dessert, sprinkle some of the crushed cookies over each serving of ice cream. Spoon warm caramel sauce on top. Serve.

Jamaican Black Bean and Vegetable Soup
Single serving is ¹/₄ of the total recipe

CALORIES 148; PROTEIN 6g; CARBS 23g;
TOTAL FAT 6g; SAT FAT 2g; CHOLESTEROL 7mg;
SODIUM 326mg; FIBER 6g

pasta and bean soup

watercress salad with fennel
crusty italian bread
spiced plum compote
with butter cookies

menu
gameplan

shopping list

Red pepper

Cannellini beans

Red kidney beans

Small shaped pasta, such as elbows or shells

Diced tomatoes

Prepared pesto sauce

Canned plums in syrup

Dry red wine or medium port wine

Orange

Butter cookies

Watercress

Fennel bulb

Lemon (for juice)

Crusty Italian bread

from your pantry

Onion

Garlic

Extra virgin olive oil

Salt and pepper

Grated Parmesan cheese (optional)

Ground cinnamon

serves 4

step **1** make the **pasta and bean soup**

step **2** make the **spiced plum compote**

step **3** assemble the **watercress salad with fennel**

step **4** **serve**

luckyforyou Stirring pesto into the soup just before serving adds instant spark. If you want the flavor of basil but not from pesto, just make the soup with the diced canned tomatoes that have basil, garlic, and oregano added.

"I am constantly amazed at how easy this soup is to put together. The ingredients are all straightforward."

—minutemeals' Chef Amanda

step 1

make the **pasta and bean soup**

1 medium onion

1 cup chopped red pepper (1 small-to-medium)

2 garlic cloves

1 can (15 ounces) cannellini beans

1 can (15 ounces) red kidney beans

1 tablespoon olive oil

3 cups water

1 cup small shaped pasta, such as elbows or shells

1/2 teaspoon salt

1/4 teaspoon cracked black pepper

1 can (14 1/2 ounces) diced tomatoes

2 tablespoons prepared pesto sauce

Grated Parmesan cheese for serving (optional)

1. Coarsely chop the onion. Chop the red pepper. Slice the garlic. Drain and rinse the cannellini beans and kidney beans.

2. Heat the olive oil in a large saucepan over medium-high heat. Add the onion, red pepper, and garlic and cook, stirring, until slightly softened, about 3 minutes. Stir in the water, beans, pasta, salt, and pepper. Increase the heat to high and bring to a boil, covered. Cook for 5 minutes.

3. Add the tomatoes and return to a boil, covered. Reduce the heat to medium and cook until the pasta is *al dente*, about 7 minutes. Stir in the pesto. Keep warm, covered.

step 2

make the **spiced plum compote**

2 cans (15 ounces each) plums in syrup

2 tablespoons dry red wine or medium port wine

One 2-inch strip orange peel, removed with a vegetable peeler

Pinch of ground cinnamon

Butter cookies

Drain 1 can of plums. Put the drained plums and the remaining can of plums with their syrup in a medium saucepan. Add the wine, orange peel, and cinnamon. Bring just to a simmer over medium heat. Reduce the heat to low and simmer until the flavors are blended and the plums are heated through. Remove from the heat, cover, and let stand until ready to serve.

step 3

assemble the **watercress salad with fennel**

2 bunches of watercress

1 small fennel bulb

Juice of 1 large lemon

3 tablespoons extra virgin olive oil

Salt and pepper to taste

1. Rinse the watercress well, remove the tough stems, and spin dry. Place in a large salad bowl.

2. Trim the fennel. Slice in half and cut out the hard core. Slice thinly and add to watercress. Add the lemon juice, olive oil, and salt and pepper and toss well.

step 4

serve

1. Divide the soup among 4 large soup bowls and place on the table. Serve Parmesan cheese for sprinkling over the soup, if desired.

2. Divide the salad among 4 salad plates and place on the table.

3. Place the bread on a bread board on the table.

4. When ready for dessert, spoon the plum compote into 4 dessert bowls, dividing it and the syrup equally. Serve with the butter cookies as an accompaniment.

Pasta and Bean Soup
Single serving is 1/4 of the total recipe
CALORIES 224; PROTEIN 8g; CARBS 32g; TOTAL FAT 7g; SAT FAT 1g; CHOLESTEROL 6mg; SODIUM 906mg; FIBER 6g

hearty tomato soup
with chickpeas

green salad with
marinated vegetables

whole-wheat pita triangles

chocolate ice pops

shopping list

Diced tomatoes with
basil and garlic

Chickpeas

Carrot

Celery

Prepared pesto

Prewashed spring or
baby greens, prewashed
spinach, or other ready-to-
serve salad mixture

Marinated vegetables,
such as mushrooms or
artichoke hearts (jarred or
from the salad bar)

Whole-wheat pita bread

Chocolate ice pops

from your pantry

Onion

Extra virgin olive oil

Cumin seeds

Pre-chopped garlic

Vegetable broth

Salt and pepper

Grated Parmesan cheese or
shredded or diced mozzarella

Red wine vinegar

serves 4

beforeyoustart

Preheat the oven to 400°F to heat the
pita triangles.

step **1** make the **hearty
tomato soup with
chickpeas**

step **2** assemble the **salad**

step **3** prepare the
**whole-wheat
pita triangles**

step **4** **serve**

luckyforyou Keep this soup interesting
no matter how many times
you serve it: Add Tabasco sauce for some heat. Swirl
diced mozzarella into the hot soup instead of dusting
it with Parmesan. Or use pre-shredded mozzarella for
similar but different effect.

"I love this menu because it was one of the first I ever developed for minutemeals. It's my idea of the perfect Sunday night supper."

—minutemeals' Chef Nancy

make the **hearty tomato soup with chickpeas**

2 cans (14¹/₂ ounces each) diced tomatoes with basil and garlic

1 can (19 ounces) chickpeas

1 large onion

1 large carrot

1 celery stalk with leaves

2 tablespoons olive oil

1 tablespoon cumin seeds

2 teaspoons pre-chopped garlic, or more to taste

4 cups vegetable broth or water, plus additional if desired

2 to 3 tablespoons prepared pesto

Salt and pepper to taste

Grated Parmesan cheese or shredded or diced mozzarella for serving

1. Drain the tomatoes. Rinse and drain the chickpeas.

2. Chop the onion to measure 1¹/₂ to 2 cups. Slice the carrot to measure ³/₄ cup. Slice the celery, including the leaves, to measure ¹/₂ cup.

3. In a large saucepan, heat the olive oil over medium-high heat until hot. Add the onion, carrot, and celery and cook, stirring often, about 3 minutes, until slightly softened. Stir in the cumin seeds and cook until fragrant, about 1 minute.

4. Add the garlic, vegetable broth or water, tomatoes, and chickpeas and stir to combine. Cover and bring to a boil over high heat. Reduce the heat to medium and simmer for 5 minutes.

step 2

assemble the **green salad with marinated vegetables**

About 6 cups prewashed spring or baby greens, prewashed spinach, or other ready-to-serve salad mixture

Marinated vegetables, such as mushrooms or artichoke hearts (jarred or from the salad bar)

1 tablespoon extra virgin olive oil

1 to 2 teaspoons red wine vinegar

Salt and pepper to taste

1. Place the greens in a salad bowl and top with the marinated vegetables.

2. Add olive oil, vinegar, and salt and pepper and toss gently, spooning the marinated vegetables back to the top of the greens. Place the bowl on the table with 4 salad plates.

step 3

prepare the **whole-wheat pita triangles**

4 to 6 whole-wheat pita breads

1. Preheat the oven to 400°F.

2. Stack the pita breads. With a sharp knife, cut them into quarters. Place the triangles on a cookie sheet and heat about 5 minutes. Transfer to a napkin-lined basket, cover, and place on the table.

step 4

serve

1. Stir the pesto into the soup and season with salt and pepper. Ladle the soup into 4 large soup bowls and serve at once, with grated Parmesan cheese to be added at the table.

2. When ready for dessert, serve the ice pops directly from the freezer.

Hearty Tomato Soup with Chickpeas
Single serving is ¹/₄ of the total recipe

CALORIES 315; PROTEIN 11g; CARBS 42g; TOTAL FAT 11g; SAT FAT 0g; CHOLESTEROL 0mg; SODIUM 896mg; FIBER 3g

★ carrot and potato soup

toasted cheese and red pepper sandwiches

three-melon fruit bowl and lemon bars

menu
gameplan

serves 4

shopping list

"Just add milk" frozen mashed potatoes

Light cream or half-and-half

Jarred roasted red peppers

Swiss, Havarti, or other favorite cheese, thinly sliced

Lemon bars

from the salad bar

Chopped scallions

Shredded carrots (or from the produce department)

Cut-up assorted melon, such as honeydew, cantaloupe, and watermelon

from your pantry

Butter

Vegetable broth

Salt and pepper

Sliced whole-wheat or rye bread

step	1	make the **carrot and potato soup**
step	2	meanwhile, make the **sandwiches**
step	3	**serve**

headsup

The soup recipe calls for the type of frozen mashed potatoes that are labeled "just add milk." If you have another type of prepared mashed potatoes (frozen or leftover home-made), you can substitute 1 cup for the 1½ cups called for in the recipe.

"Company coming? Jazz up the soup garnish by offering small bowls of raisins, toasted nuts such as pecans or pine nuts, and toasted coconut."

—minutemeals' Chef Ruth

step 1

make the **carrot and potato soup**

3 tablespoons butter

1 1/2 cups chopped scallions

10 ounces (about 4 cups) shredded carrots

2 cans (14 1/2 ounces each) vegetable broth (about 4 cups)

1 1/2 cups cups "just add milk" frozen mashed potatoes

1/2 cup light cream or half-and-half

Salt and pepper to taste

1. Melt the butter in a 3-quart non-stick saucepan over medium heat. Add 1 cup of the scallions and cook, stirring, until nearly tender, about 2 minutes.

2. Add the carrots and broth. Cover, increase the heat to high, and bring to a boil. Reduce the heat to medium and simmer for 5 minutes, or until the carrots are almost tender.

3. Stir in the potatoes, cover, and cook for 5 minutes.

step 2

meanwhile, make the **toasted cheese and red pepper sandwiches**

1 jar (7 ounces) roasted red peppers

8 slices whole-wheat or rye bread

3 tablespoons softened butter

8 ounces thinly sliced Swiss, Havarti, or other favorite cheese

1. Drain the red peppers well and cut into thin strips.

2. Spread 1 side of each bread slice lightly with butter. Top unbuttered sides of 4 of the bread slices with cheese and pepper strips; cover with a bread slice, buttered side up.

3. Heat a large range-top grill pan or griddle or nonstick skillet over medium-high heat. Place the sandwiches on the grill, in batches if necessary, and toast until both sides are evenly golden brown and the cheese is melted, pressing down lightly with spatula. Transfer to a cutting board.

step 3

serve

1. While the sandwiches are grilling, transfer the soup mixture to a blender or food processor and puree until smooth, working in batches if necessary. Return the soup to the saucepan and stir in the light cream or half-and-half. Season with salt and pepper. Heat until steaming.

2. Ladle the soup into soup bowls and garnish each with some of the remaining 1/2 cup chopped scallions. Serve.

3. Cut the sandwiches in half or quarters and serve on small plates with the soup.

4. When ready for dessert, divide the cut-up melon among 4 dessert bowls. Place the lemon bars on a serving plate and pass at the table.

Carrot and Potato Soup
Single serving is 1/4 of the total recipe

CALORIES 245; PROTEIN 5g; CARBS 34g;
TOTAL FAT 11g; SAT FAT 7g; CHOLESTEROL 31mg;
SODIUM 124mg; FIBER 5g

cheese tortellini and yogurt soup
tomato and olive salad
rosemary focaccia
fresh grapes

menu
gameplan

serves 4

shopping list

Fresh parsley

Fresh mint

Fresh cheese-filled tricolor tortellini

Plain low-fat yogurt

Ripe tomatoes

Brine-cured black olives, pitted

Rosemary focaccia

Grapes (from the salad bar or produce department)

from your pantry

Onion

Fruity olive oil

All-purpose flour

Vegetable broth

Salt and pepper

step 1   make the **cheese tortellini and yogurt soup**

step 2   assemble the **tomato and olive salad**

step 3   **serve**

headsup Really be sure to follow our directions as to how the yogurt is incorporated into the soup base right before serving: Broth is added to the yogurt, not vice versa. The way we've done it ensures that the soup does not curdle—a risk if you reverse the order and stir yogurt into very hot soup.

"This soup is a variation of an Armenian favorite made with barley. For those dog days of summer, try it served chilled." —minutemeals' Chef Paul

make the **cheese tortellini and yogurt soup**

- 1 medium onion
- 5 tablespoons combined chopped fresh parsley and mint
- 1 tablespoon fruity olive oil
- 1 tablespoon all-purpose flour
- 1 can (14 1/2 ounces) vegetable broth
- 2 cups water
- 8 ounces fresh cheese-filled tricolor tortellini
- Salt and pepper to taste
- 1 pint plain low-fat yogurt

1. Coarsely chop the onion. Chop enough parsley and mint to measure 5 tablespoons combined. Set 3 tablespoons aside for this recipe.

2. In a large heavy saucepan, cook the onion in the olive oil over medium-high heat, stirring, for 4 minutes, or until just starting to soften.

3. Stir in the flour until blended. Add the vegetable broth and water, cover, and bring to a boil over high heat.

4. Add the tortellini and the 3 tablespoons chopped herbs and bring to a simmer. Cover and cook for 12 minutes, or until the tortellini are just tender. Remove the pan from the heat and season the soup with salt and pepper.

step 2

assemble the **tomato and olive salad**

- 3 large ripe tomatoes
- 1/3 cup pitted brine-cured black olives
- 2 tablespoons chopped combined fresh parsley and mint (prepped above)
- 1 tablespoon fruity olive oil
- Salt and pepper to taste

1. Rinse the tomatoes, pat dry, and cut into 3/4-inch pieces. Place in a medium shallow serving dish.

2. Coarsely chop the olives and scatter them over the tomatoes. Sprinkle the herbs on top, then drizzle with the olive oil. Season with salt and pepper. Place the dish on the table, with 4 salad plates.

step 3

serve

1. Spoon the yogurt for the soup into a 1 1/2-quart serving bowl. Add a ladle of the hot broth from the soup and stir until blended. Stir in the remaining soup. Ladle the soup into 4 large soup bowls and serve.

2. Place the focaccia on a bread board and serve, if desired, with a small bowl of olive oil for dipping.

3. When ready for dessert, place the grapes in a basket or bowl and serve.

Cheese Tortellini and Yogurt Soup
Single serving is 1/4 of the total recipe

CALORIES 300; PROTEIN 15g; CARBS 41g;
TOTAL FAT 9g; SAT FAT 2g; CHOLESTEROL 30mg;
SODIUM 324mg; FIBER 3g

soup and stew menus • 49

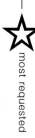
☆ chinese dumpling and bok choy soup

snow pea and grape tomato salad

italian lemon ices

menu
gameplan

shopping list

Bok choy

Cilantro

Gingerroot

Oriental-style frozen
vegetable dumplings

Shredded carrots
(from the salad bar or from
the produce department)

Oriental-style vinaigrette

Black beans

Grape tomatoes

Snow peas

Italian lemon ices

from your pantry

Vegetable broth

Lite soy sauce

Toasted sesame oil

serves 4

beforeyoustart

Place the lemon ices in the refrigerator to soften, if desired.

step 1 make the **chinese dumpling and bok choy soup**

step 2 assemble the **snow pea and grape tomato salad**

step 3 **serve**

headsup Look for frozen Oriental dumplings in specialty food stores, including Asian produce markets. When you find them, buy several bags.

"If your supermarket does not stock the Oriental-style dumplings that are called for, substitute fresh cheese-filled tortellini, cooking them until tender."

—minutemeals' Chef Paul

make the **chinese dumpling and bok choy soup**

- 5 large stalks bok choy
- 3 tablespoons chopped cilantro
- 1½ teaspoons grated fresh gingerroot
- 4 cups water
- 1 can (14½ ounces) vegetable broth
- 16 Oriental-style frozen vegetable dumplings (about 12 ounces)
- 1 cup shredded carrots
- 2 tablespoons lite soy sauce
- 2 teaspoons toasted sesame oil

1. Rinse the bok choy, pat dry, and slice enough of both the stems and the leaves ¼ inch thick to measure 4 cups. Rinse the cilantro and chop enough to measure 3 tablespoons. Grate enough ginger to measure 1½ teaspoons.

2. Pour the water and vegetable broth into a large saucepan, cover, and bring to a boil over high heat. Add the sliced bok choy, cover, and simmer for 6 minutes.

3. Stir in the dumplings, carrots, soy sauce, and ginger. Bring to a simmer, cover, and cook for 2 to 3 minutes, or until the dumplings are just tender. Do not overcook.

assemble the **snow pea and grape tomato salad**

- 2 tablespoons chopped cilantro
- ¼ cup store-bought Oriental-style vinaigrette
- 1 cup canned black beans
- 1 cup grape tomatoes
- 6 ounces fresh snow peas

1. Chop enough cilantro to measure 2 tablespoons. Place in a medium serving bowl, add the vinaigrette, and stir to combine.

2. Rinse the grape tomatoes and pat dry. Rinse the black beans, drain, and shake dry. Add the tomatoes and the beans to the bowl and toss.

3. String the snow peas. Bring 1 cup water to a boil, covered, in a medium skillet. Add the snow peas and blanch for 30 seconds. Drain and reserve.

serve

1. Stir the sesame oil into the soup and top with the chopped cilantro. Ladle into 4 bowls, allowing 4 dumplings per person. Serve.

2. Add the snow peas to the salad and toss to combine. Place the bowl on the table, with 4 salad plates.

3. When ready for dessert, place each lemon ice to a small dessert bowl and serve.

Chinese Dumpling and Bok Choy Soup
Single serving is ¼ of the total recipe

CALORIES 469; PROTEIN 16g; CARBS 88g;
TOTAL FAT 5g; SAT FAT 1g; CHOLESTEROL 12mg;
SODIUM 1081mg; FIBER 6g

corn chowder
cheese and chile quesadillas
warm nectarines with vanilla ice cream

menu
gameplan

shopping list

Frozen corn kernels

Canned cream-style corn

Ripe nectarines

Vanilla ice cream

Flour tortillas
(6- to 7-inch diameter)

Pre-shredded Monterey Jack cheese

Canned chopped mild green chiles or sliced pickled jalapeños

Salsa, mild or spicy

from your pantry

Onion

Butter

Salt and pepper

Milk

Light brown sugar

Ground cinnamon

Ground cloves

serves 4

beforeyoustart
Preheat the broiler.

step 1 make the **corn chowder**

step 2 prepare the **warm nectarines with vanilla ice cream**

step 3 make the **cheese and chile quesadillas**

step 4 **serve**

luckyforyou
As anyone who has ever grated soft cheese knows, it takes time and can be messy. Monterey Jack, fortunately, is sold pre-grated or pre-shredded in resealable bags. It's a convenience that's well worth the investment.

make the **corn chowder**

1 large onion

1 tablespoon butter

1 package (10 ounces) frozen corn kernels

1/2 teaspoon salt

1/4 teaspoon pepper

3 cups whole milk

1 can (16 ounces) cream-style corn

1. Finely chop the onion.

2. In a large saucepan, melt the butter over medium-high heat. Add the onion and cook, stirring, until slightly softened, about 3 minutes. Stir in the frozen corn and salt and pepper and cook 2 to 3 minutes, until heated through.

3. Stir in the milk and creamed corn. Bring to a boil, covered, over medium-high heat, stirring frequently. Reduce the heat to medium-low and simmer the soup gently for 5 minutes. Remove the pan from the heat, but keep warm, covered.

prepare the **warm nectarines with vanilla ice cream**

4 large ripe nectarines

3 tablespoons light brown sugar

Pinch of ground cinnamon

Pinch of ground cloves

Vanilla ice cream for serving

1. Preheat the broiler.

2. Cut the nectarines in half and remove the pits. Place, cut side up, in a shallow baking dish. Sprinkle with the brown sugar and spices. Broil 6 inches from the heat for 2 minutes, until the topping is heated and bubbly. Transfer each nectarine half to a dessert bowl and keep warm, loosely covered. Keep the broiler on for the quesadillas.

make the **cheese and chile quesadillas**

4 flour tortillas (6- to 7-inch diameter)

1 1/2 cups pre-shredded Monterey Jack cheese

1 can (4 1/2 ounces) chopped mild green chiles or 1/4 cup sliced pickled jalapeños

Mild or spicy salsa for serving

1. Place the tortillas on 1 or 2 large cookie sheets. Sprinkle each with some of the cheese and some of the chiles, drained. Broil for 2 to 3 minutes, or until the cheese is melted and bubbly. Cut each tortilla into wedges and arrange around the rim of a large platter.

2. Spoon the salsa into a small serving bowl and place in the middle of the platter. Place the platter on the table.

serve

1. Ladle the chowder, dividing it equally, among 4 large soup bowls. Serve with the quesadillas and salsa.

2. When ready for dessert, top each nectarine half with a scoop of the vanilla ice cream and serve.

Corn Chowder
Single serving is 1/4 of the total recipe
CALORIES 253; PROTEIN 9g; CARBS 35g;
TOTAL FAT 10g; SAT FAT 6g; CHOLESTEROL 34mg;
SODIUM 587mg; FIBER 2g

potato soup
with watercress

beets with blue cheese on baby greens

ladyfingers with coffee sorbet and whipped cream

serves 4

shopping list

Leeks

Frozen grated hash brown potatoes

Watercress or arugula sprigs or baby spinach leaves

Prewashed spring or baby greens

Pickled beets

Blue cheese

Coffee sorbet or ice cream

Ladyfingers

Instant whipped cream

from your pantry

Butter

Vegetable broth

Salt and pepper

Extra virgin olive oil

Red wine vinegar

step **1** make the **potato soup with watercress**

step **2** assemble the **beets with blue cheese on baby greens**

step **3** Prepare the **ladyfingers**

step **4** **serve**

luckyforyou The dessert here is a quick take on Italy's famous cake-with-custard creation, tiramisu. If ladyfingers aren't available at your market, sponge cake makes a fine substitute.

make the **potato soup with watercress**

2 large leeks

6 tablespoons butter

2 cans (14¹/2 ounces each) vegetable broth

2 cups water

4¹/2 cups packed frozen grated hash brown potatoes (1¹/2 pounds Russet or baking potatoes)

1 large bunch of watercress or arugula sprigs or baby spinach leaves

Salt and pepper to taste

1. Slice the tough green leaves from the leeks and discard. Slice each leek in half lengthwise just up to but not through the root end. Rinse the leeks well under cold running water, fanning out the leaves. Place each leek cut side down and thinly slice.

2. In a Dutch oven, melt the butter over medium-high heat. Add the leeks and cook, stirring, until nearly soft, about 5 minutes. Reduce the heat if they begin to brown.

3. Stir in the vegetable broth, water, and grated potatoes. Cover, increase the heat to high, and bring the liquid to a boil. Lower the heat so that the mixture simmers and partially cover. Cook for 7 minutes.

4. Remove the tough stems from the watercress and discard. Rinse the leaves and tender stems, pat dry, and finely chop.

assemble the **beets with blue cheese on baby greens**

1 bag (5 to 7 ounces) prewashed spring or baby greens

1 jar (15 to 16 ounces) pickled beets

3 ounces crumbled blue cheese

3 tablespoons extra virgin olive oil

1 tablespoon red wine vinegar

Salt and pepper to taste

1. Divide the greens among 4 salad plates.

2. Drain the beets and arrange on the greens. Divide the blue cheese among the salads, scattering it over the beets.

3. In a cup, with a fork, mix the olive oil and vinegar. Season with salt and pepper. Spoon the dressing over the salads and place them on the table.

prepare the **ladyfingers with coffee sorbet and whipped cream**

1 pint coffee sorbet or ice cream

8 ladyfingers

Instant whipped cream

1. Remove the sorbet or ice cream from the freezer to soften during dinner.

2. Arrange 2 ladyfingers in each dessert bowl.

serve

1. Stir the watercress and salt and pepper to taste into the hot soup. Ladle into 4 large soup bowls and place on the table.

2. When ready for dessert, place a scoop of the sorbet on the ladyfingers in each dessert bowl. Garnish with whipped cream and serve.

Potato Soup with Watercress
Single serving is ¹/4 of the total recipe
CALORIES 380; PROTEIN 4g; CARBS 51g;
TOTAL FAT 19g; SAT FAT 0g; CHOLESTEROL 45mg;
SODIUM 70mg; FIBER 6g

squash soup
with toasted pine nuts
rondelé wraps
apricots with gingersnaps

shopping list

Pine nuts (*pignoli*)

Apple

Frozen squash

Flour tortillas
(8- to 9-inch diameter)

Plum tomatoes

Garlic-and-herb-flavored
rondelé cheese spread

Apricot halves packed
in syrup

Gingersnaps

from the salad bar

Spinach leaves

Thin cucumber slices

from your pantry

Yellow onion

Butter

Dried sage

Vegetable broth

Salt and pepper

serves 4

beforeyoustart

Preheat the oven to 375°F to toast the
pine nuts. Chill the apricots, if desired,
until serving time.

| step | 1 | make the **squash soup with toasted pine nuts** |

| step | 2 | assemble **rondelé wraps** |

| step | 3 | **serve** |

headsup We've called for heating the
tortillas for the wraps briefly in
the microwave to soften them. It's an extra step, but
shouldn't be skirted in the interests of time or for lack of a
microwave. If you don't have a microwave, just pop the
tortillas into the preheated conventional oven after you
toast the pine nuts.

"I love this after Thanksgiving. It's seasonal but light, just what you want when you feel as if you've been cooking and eating for days."

—minutemeals' Chef Ruth

step 1

make the **squash soup with toasted pine nuts**

1/2 cup pine nuts

1 small yellow onion

1 small apple

2 tablespoons butter

1 teaspoon dried sage

1 package (12 ounces) frozen cooked squash

3 cups vegetable broth

Salt and pepper to taste

1. Preheat the oven to 375°F. Spread the pine nuts in a small baking dish.

2. Finely chop the onion to measure about 1/2 cup. Peel, core, and grate the apple.

3. Melt the butter in a 3-quart saucepan over medium heat. Add the onion, apple, and sage and cook, stirring frequently, until the onion is slightly softened.

4. Add the frozen squash and vegetable broth to the pan. Cover, increase the heat to high, and bring the mixture to a boil. Reduce the heat to medium-low and simmer, covered, stirring occasionally, about 5 minutes, or until the squash is thawed.

5. While soup is cooking, toast the pine nuts in the oven, stirring occasionally, for about 5 minutes, or until lightly toasted. Do not let overbrown. Remove and let cool.

step 2

assemble **rondelé wraps**

4 plum tomatoes

4 flour tortillas (8- to 9-inch diameter)

1 package (4 ounces) garlic-and-herb-flavored rondelé cheese spread

8 to 10 large spinach leaves

1 cup thin cucumber slices

1. Heat the tortillas in the microwave oven according to the directions on the package until softened slightly and pliable. Remove to the work surface.

2. Slice plum tomatoes. Spread each tortilla with a generous amount of the rondelé. Top the cheese with spinach leaves, a layer of cucumber slices, and finally a layer of tomato slices. Roll each tortilla up to form a wrap and place seam side down on a serving plate. Place the plate on the table, with 4 serving plates.

step 3

serve

1. If you prefer a smooth-textured soup, carefully ladle the soup into a food processor or blender and puree until smooth; pour the puree into the saucepan and season with salt and pepper. Or, ladle the soup into 4 large soup bowls and season. Sprinkle the servings with toasted pine nuts and serve.

2. When ready for dessert, divide the apricot halves with some of their syrup among small dessert bowls and serve with the gingersnaps, or crumble the gingersnaps over the top, and serve.

Squash Soup with Toasted Pine Nuts
Single serving is 1/4 of the total recipe
CALORIES 239; PROTEIN 6g; CARBS 24g;
TOTAL FAT 15g; SAT FAT 5g; CHOLESTEROL 16mg;
SODIUM 117mg; FIBER 2g

artichoke and mushroom stew

black-eyed pea salad with corn and red peppers
dessert waffles with strawberries and cream

shopping list

Presliced mushrooms
(from the produce department)

Frozen artichoke hearts

Sour cream, light or regular

Canned corn kernels

Basil leaves

Sliced roasted red peppers

Black-eyed peas

Quick-thaw frozen
strawberries

Toaster waffles

Instant light whipped cream

Thin onion slices
(from the salad bar)

from your pantry

Butter

All-purpose flour

Vegetable broth

Salt and pepper

Balsamic vinaigrette

serves 4

beforeyoustart

Thaw the frozen artichoke hearts in
the microwave oven according to the
directions on the package.

step 1 make the **artichoke and mushroom stew**

step 2 assemble **salad**

step 3 prepare the **dessert waffles**

step 4 **serve**

luckyforyou There's not one difficult-to-find ingredient in this
entire menu. Stock the canned or frozen items in advance,
which will leave you only the fresh produce to buy—
a total of 3 ingredients.

"This stew makes the perfect dinner on a blustery night, but it's also great for brunch, served over halved croissants or toast points."

—minutemeals' Chef Nancy

step 1

make the **artichoke and mushroom stew**

3 tablespoons butter

2 cups thin onion slices

2 boxes (8 ounces each) presliced mushrooms

2 tablespoons all-purpose flour

2 cups vegetable broth

2 boxes (9 ounces each) frozen artichoke hearts, thawed

1 cup light or regular sour cream

Salt and pepper to taste

1. In a Dutch oven or a large deep skillet, melt the butter over medium-high heat. Add the onions and cook, stirring often, until nearly tender, about 2 minutes.

2. Add the mushrooms, stir just to combine, and increase the heat to high. Cover and cook, stirring often, until the mushrooms are soft and tender, about 4 minutes. Add the flour and cook, stirring and scraping the bottom of the pan, for 1 minute.

3. Add the broth, cover, and bring to a boil, scraping the bottom and sides of the pan. Add the artichoke hearts and bring to a boil, covered. Reduce the heat to medium, cover, and simmer, stirring occasionally, until serving time.

step 2

assemble the **black-eyed pea salad with corn and red peppers**

1 can (16 ounces) corn kernels

7 leaves fresh basil

1/2 cup sliced roasted red peppers

1 can (15 to 16 ounces) black-eyed peas

2 to 3 tablespoons balsamic vinaigrette

Salt and pepper to taste

1. Drain the corn. Rinse the basil leaves, pat dry, and tear into pieces.

2. In a salad bowl, combine the corn, roasted peppers, and black-eyed peas. Add the basil and vinaigrette. Season with salt and pepper and toss to coat. Place the bowl, with 4 salad plates, on the table.

step 3

prepare the **dessert waffles with strawberries and cream**

1 bag (12 ounces) quick-thaw frozen strawberries

4 toaster waffles

Instant light whipped cream

Thaw the strawberries in the microwave oven according to the directions on the package.

step 4

serve

1. Remove the artichoke and mushroom stew from the heat and stir in the sour cream until combined. Season with salt and pepper. Ladle the stew into soup or pasta bowls and place on the table. Serve with the salad or follow it with the salad.

2. When ready for dessert, toast the waffles according to the directions on the package. To serve, place a waffle on each of 4 dessert plates. Top with strawberries and some of their syrup. Garnish with whipped cream and serve, with additional whipped cream, if desired.

Artichoke and Mushroom Stew
Single serving is 1/4 of the total recipe
CALORIES 225; PROTEIN 7g; CARBS 22g;
TOTAL FAT 14g; SAT FAT 6g; CHOLESTEROL 33mg;
SODIUM 235mg; FIBER 6g

avgolemono stew
(lemon and egg soup with chickpeas and spinach)

tomato and feta salad

sesame breadsticks

baklava

menu **gameplan**

serves 4

shopping list

Chickpeas

Shredded carrots
(from the salad bar or from
the produce department)

Lemons (for juice)

Prewashed baby spinach

Ripe tomatoes

Feta cheese

Sesame breadsticks

Baklava

from your pantry

Vegetable broth

Long-grain white rice

Eggs

Salt and pepper

Dried oregano or
fresh oregano leaves

Extra virgin olive oil

Red wine vinegar

lucky**foryou** Tired of spinach? Other
greens work well in the
stew, including Swiss chard leaves (no ribs included),
arugula, or escarole.

"Be careful finishing the soup—following the directions will keep it from becoming egg drop soup!"

—minutemeals' Chef Nancy

step 1

make the **avgolemono stew**

4 cups vegetable broth

1 can (15 ounces) chickpeas, undrained

1/3 cup long-grain white rice

1 cup shredded carrots

2 large eggs

2 to 3 tablespoons fresh lemon juice (2 lemons)

1 bag (4 to 5 ounces) prewashed baby spinach

Salt and pepper to taste

1. In a large saucepan or Dutch oven, combine the vegetable broth, chickpeas with their liquid, and rice. Cover and bring to a boil over high heat.

2. Stir in the carrots and reduce the heat so that the liquid boils gently. Cover and cook until the rice is tender but slightly firm to the bite, about 10 minutes.

step 2

assemble the **tomato and feta salad**

4 ripe medium tomatoes

6 ounces feta cheese

1/2 teaspoon dried oregano or 1 tablespoon chopped fresh oregano leaves

3 tablespoons extra virgin olive oil

1 tablespoon red wine vinegar

Salt and pepper to taste

1. Rinse the tomatoes and pat dry. Cut into thin wedges. Arrange the wedges on a platter.

2. Crumble the feta over the tomatoes. Sprinkle the oregano, crushing it with your fingers, over all. Drizzle the oil and vinegar over the salad and season with salt and pepper. Place the platter on the table, with 4 salad plates.

step 3

serve

1. Finish the stew: In a small bowl, with a fork, beat the eggs lightly. Add 2 to 3 tablespoons lemon juice and stir to combine.

2. Remove the stew from the heat. Ladle 1/2 cup of the hot liquid into the eggs and stir immediately to prevent the eggs from setting. Stirring, pour the egg-lemon-broth mixture into the stew and place the pan over low heat. Add the spinach, stirring until wilted. (It will wilt almost immediately upon contact with the hot liquid.) Remove the pan from the heat and season with salt and pepper.

3. Ladle the stew into 4 large soup bowls. Serve, with the sesame breadsticks and salad.

4. When ready for dessert, place a piece of baklava on each of 4 dessert plates and serve.

Avgolemono Stew
Single serving is 1/4 of the total recipe
CALORIES 263; PROTEIN 15g; CARBS 39g; TOTAL FAT 6g; SAT FAT 1g; CHOLESTEROL 120mg; SODIUM 159mg; FIBER 12g

green chili
baked corn chips
zucchini and carrot ribbon slaw
caramel custards

menu gameplan

shopping list

Corn tortillas
(7-inch diameter)

Cilantro

Great Northern or white beans

Canned chopped mild green chiles

Sour cream

Zucchini

Carrots

Caramel custards

from your pantry

Vegetable cooking spray

Salt and pepper

Onion

Dried oregano

Extra virgin olive oil

Red wine vinegar

serves 4

beforeyoustart

Preheat the oven to 400°F to bake the corn chips.

step 1 make the **baked corn chips**

step 2 make the **green chili**

step 3 prepare the **zucchini and carrot ribbon slaw**

step 4 **serve**

headsup A Y-shaped vegetable peeler will cut the vegetables for the slaw into wide ribbons. Look for it in any kitchenware store. A regular vegetable peeler will work, too, just make sure that it's sharp.

"I really like red chili but when I want a change of pace, green chili is what I make. It's really fresh-tasting, totally different." —minutemeals' Chef Nancy

step 1

make the **baked corn chips**

1 package (9 1/2 ounces) corn tortillas (7-inch diameter)

Vegetable cooking spray

Salt to taste

1. Preheat the oven to 400°F.

2. Stack the tortillas and cut them into quarters. Place the tortilla pieces in one layer on a large cookie sheet, spray with vegetable oil, and sprinkle with salt. Bake about 10 minutes, until the pieces are starting to crisp and are lightly colored. Transfer to a napkin-lined basket and place the basket on the table.

step 2

make the **green chili**

1 medium-large onion

1/2 cup coarsely chopped packed cilantro

3 tablespoons olive oil

2 teaspoons dried oregano

2 cans (15 ounces each) Great Northern or white beans, undrained

2 cans (4 1/2 ounces each) chopped mild green chiles, undrained

1 cup water

4 tablespoons sour cream for serving

1. Coarsely chop the onion to measure 2 cups. Rinse, pat dry, then coarsely chop leaves and some of the tender stems of enough cilantro sprigs to measure 1/2 cup packed.

2. Heat the olive oil in a large saucepan over medium-high heat until hot. Stir in the onion and oregano and cook until the onion is nearly tender, about 3 minutes.

3. Add the beans and chiles, both undrained, plus the water to the pan, stir to combine, and bring to a boil, covered. Reduce the heat and simmer for 5 minutes. Remove from the heat and keep warm, covered.

step 3

prepare the **zucchini and carrot ribbon slaw**

2 small-to-medium zucchini

2 medium carrots

3 tablespoons extra virgin olive oil

1 tablespoon red wine vinegar

Salt and pepper to taste

1. Rinse the zucchini and carrots and pat dry. Hold the stem end of one of the zucchini. With a sharp potato peeler, preferably a Y-shaped peeler, shred the zucchini in long, thin ribbon-like strips. Shred just down to the seedy core of the zucchini and discard the core. Repeat

with the remaining zucchini. Shred the carrots in the same manner until you have only a small piece of stem end left.

2. Place the vegetable strips in a bowl, add the olive oil, vinegar, and salt and pepper, and toss to coat. Pile the slaw on a serving platter and place the platter on the table, with 4 salad plates.

step 4

serve

1. Ladle the chili into 4 soup or pasta bowls. Top each with 1 tablespoon of sour cream.

2. Serve the corn chips for sprinkling over the chili or as an accompaniment.

3. When ready for dessert, place a custard in each of 4 dessert bowls and serve.

Green Chili
Single serving is 1/4 of the total recipe
CALORIES 251; PROTEIN 10g; CARBS 33g; TOTAL FAT 14g; SAT FAT 4g; CHOLESTEROL 10mg; SODIUM 827mg; FIBER 11g

☆ chili primavera
scallion rice
warm corn muffins
strawberries with lime syrup

menu
gameplan

serves 4

shopping list
Red pepper

Pinto or kidney beans

Zucchini

Chili-style stewed tomatoes

Shredded carrots
(from the salad bar or from
the produce department)

Frozen corn

Salsa, medium-spicy or hot

Pre-shredded Cheddar or
Monterey Jack cheese

Chopped scallions
(from the salad bar)

Limes (for juice)

Ripe strawberries

Corn muffins

from your pantry
Onion

Olive oil

Salt

Instant white rice

Sugar

step	1	make the **chili primavera**
step	2	prepare the **scallion rice**
step	3	prepare the **strawberries**
step	4	prepare the w**arm corn muffins**
step	5	**serve**

lucky**for**you By buying ready-to-use
items, pre-shredded carrots
and chopped scallions, you free yourself up to prep the
rest of the vegetables in the chili. If they're available at
your market, buy cut-up red pepper, too.

"When I run out of time, I serve this chili over the corn muffins. The muffin, the chili, the cheese, it makes a great bowl."

—minutemeals' Chef Amanda

step 1
make the **chili primavera**

- 1 medium red pepper
- 1 medium onion
- 1 can (19 ounces) pinto or kidney beans
- 1 medium zucchini
- 2 teaspoons olive oil
- 2 cans (14 1/2 ounces each) chili-style stewed tomatoes
- 1/2 cup water
- 1 cup shredded carrots
- 1/2 teaspoon salt
- 1 cup frozen corn kernels
- 1/2 cup medium-spicy or hot salsa
- 1 cup pre-shredded Cheddar or Monterey Jack cheese

1. Coarsely chop the red pepper and onion. Rinse and drain the beans. Thinly slice the zucchini.

2. In a 4- to 6-quart saucepan, heat the olive oil over high heat. Add the red pepper and onion and cook, stirring occasionally, until slightly softened, about 3 minutes.

3. Add the beans, tomatoes, water, carrots, and salt. Bring the mixture to a boil, covered. Reduce the heat slightly and simmer for 10 minutes.

4. Add the zucchini, corn, and salsa and stir to combine. Bring the chili to a boil, covered, reduce the heat slightly, and simmer for 5 minutes, or until the vegetables are just tender. Keep warm, covered.

step 2
prepare the **scallion rice**

- 2 cups instant white rice
- 2 cups water
- 1/2 cup chopped scallions

Prepare the rice according to the directions on the package. Stir in the chopped scallions until combined. Keep warm, covered.

step 3
prepare the **strawberries with lime syrup**

- Juice of 2 limes
- 2 tablespoons sugar
- 2 tablespoons water
- 2 pints ripe strawberries

1. Combine the lime juice, sugar, and water in a small saucepan and bring to a simmer. Cook for 5 minutes, until the sugar is dissolved. Cool.

2. Rinse and hull the berries; cut in half. Place in a bowl and let stand until serving time.

step 4
prepare the **warm corn muffins**

- 4 store-bought corn muffins

In a toaster oven, heat the corn muffins at 350°F for 5 to 7 minutes, or until warmed through. Place in a napkin-lined basket, cover to keep warm, and place the basket on the table.

step 5
serve

1. Spoon the chili into 4 large soup bowls and top each serving with some of the shredded Cheddar or Monterey Jack cheese. Serve at once.

2. Place the rice on the table. (If desired, serve the chili on the rice.)

3. When ready for dessert, divide the strawberries among dessert bowls. Drizzle lime syrup over each and serve.

Chili Primavera
Single serving is 1/4 of the total recipe
CALORIES 442; PROTEIN 23g; CARBS 57g;
TOTAL FAT 17g; SAT FAT 7g; CHOLESTEROL 30mg;
SODIUM 888mg; FIBER 9g

curried lentil and spinach stew

couscous

pear and honey-mustard salad

sugar cookies

menu
gameplan

serves 4

shopping list

Red lentils

Frozen leaf spinach

Plain low-fat yogurt

Plain couscous

Ripe pear

Prewashed Italian-style mixed salad greens

Golden raisins or dried cranberries

Sugar cookies

from the salad bar

Shredded carrots (or from the produce department)

Chopped scallions

from your pantry

Garlic

Curry powder

Salt and pepper

Olive oil

White wine vinegar

Honey mustard

beforeyoustart

Bring the water to a boil in a large saucepan, covered, over high heat for the stew.

step 1 cook the **curried lentil and spinach stew**

step 2 prepare the **couscous**

step 3 assemble the **pear and honey-mustard salad**

step 4 **serve**

headsup

Look for frozen cut-leaf spinach in bags at your super-market. Since the leaves are individually frozen, the spinach can be measured out easily. In addition, it cooks more quickly, since it's not in solid brick form.

"If you don't have honey mustard for the salad dressing, make your own by blending together equal parts of honey and Dijon mustard."

—minutemeals' Chef Paul

step 1
cook the **curried lentil and spinach stew**

1 cup red lentils

4 cups water

2 large garlic cloves

1 cup shredded carrots

1 tablespoon curry powder

2 cups frozen leaf spinach (from a 16-ounce bag)

1/2 cup chopped scallions

Salt and pepper to taste

1 container (8 ounces) plain low-fat yogurt for serving

1. Put the lentils in a fine-mesh strainer and pick them over to remove any bits of debris. Rinse the lentils and put them in a heavy saucepan. Add the water, stir, and cover. Bring to a boil over high heat.

2. Meanwhile, chop the garlic. Add the garlic to the pan, with the carrots and curry powder. Bring to a boil, covered; reduce the heat to low, and partially cover. Simmer, stirring occasionally, for 8 minutes, or until the lentils are just tender.

3. Stir in the spinach and scallions. Increase the heat to medium, cover, and cook for 2 minutes, or until the spinach is tender. Season with salt and pepper.

step 2
prepare the **couscous**

1 box (10 ounces) plain couscous

Water

Olive oil

Make the couscous according to the directions on the package. Let stand, covered, until ready to serve.

step 3
assemble the **pear and honey-mustard salad**

2 tablespoons olive oil

1 tablespoon white wine vinegar

1 tablespoon honey mustard

1 ripe large pear

1 bag (about 7 ounces) prewashed Italian-style mixed salad greens

2 tablespoons golden raisins or dried cranberries

Salt and pepper to taste

1. In a salad bowl, with a fork, whisk together the oil, vinegar, and mustard until blended.

2. Quarter the pear lengthwise and cut out the core and stem. Cut the pear into thin wedges and add to the dressing. Toss to coat.

3. Place the greens and raisins or dried cranberries on top. When ready to serve, toss until the greens are evenly coated with dressing. Season with salt and pepper. Place the salad on the table with 4 salad plates.

step 4
serve

1. Divide the stew among 4 shallow bowls and add a dollop, 2 tablespoons, of yogurt to each. Serve.

2. Fluff the couscous with a fork, transfer to a serving bowl, and serve with the lentil stew.

3. Toss the salad and serve.

4. When ready for dessert, serve the cookies on a plate.

Curried Lentil and Spinach Stew
Single serving is 1/4 of the total recipe
(includes 2 tablespoons plain lowfat yogurt)

CALORIES 240; PROTEIN 20g; CARBS 43g;
TOTAL FAT 1g; SAT FAT 0g; CHOLESTEROL 0mg;
SODIUM 186mg; FIBER 23g

minute

main-dish salad menus

corn and black bean salad
on arugula
tomatoes and cucumbers with basil oil
peanut butter chocolate chip cookies

menu gameplan

shopping list

Frozen corn kernels

Black beans

Arugula

Red onion

Cilantro

Lemons (for juice)

Ripe plum tomatoes

Cucumber

Basil oil or garlic-flavored olive oil

Oversize chocolate chip cookies

from your pantry

Olive oil

Ground cumin

Salt and pepper

Hot red pepper sauce

Peanut butter, smooth or chunky

Milk (optional)

serves 4 to 6

step 1 make the **corn and black bean salad on arugula**

step 2 assemble the **tomatoes and cucumbers with basil oil**

step 3 assemble the **peanut butter chocolate chip cookies**

step 4 **serve**

headsup

Ever been at a loss as to what to do with leftover fresh corn on the cob, the ears that didn't get snapped up hot? Here is a great option: Use it in this salad. Hold the cob upright on the work surface and with a sharp knife, cut the kernels straight off. Be careful not to let the cob slip while you're cutting.

"Flavored oils are really popular. Once you could only find them in gourmet food stores, but now they're sold in some supermarkets."

—minutemeals' Chef Hillary

step 1

make the **corn and black bean salad on arugula**

2 boxes (10 ounces each) frozen corn kernels

1 can (16 ounces) black beans

2 bunches of arugula

1 medium red onion

1/4 cup chopped cilantro

3 tablespoons olive oil

Juice of 2 lemons

1 teaspoon ground cumin

1/2 teaspoon salt

1/8 teaspoon hot red pepper sauce

1. Thaw the corn kernels in the microwave oven according to the directions on the package. Rinse and drain the black beans.

2. Trim the tough stems from the arugula; rinse the leaves, and spin dry. Place the arugula in a bowl.

3. Chop the red onion. Chop enough cilantro to measure 1/4 cup. Combine the red onion and cilantro in a medium salad bowl. Add the olive oil, lemon juice, cumin, salt, and hot red pepper sauce and stir with a fork until combined. Remove 3 tablespoons of the dressing to a cup and reserve for dressing the arugula.

4. Add the corn and beans to the salad bowl and toss to coat.

step 2

assemble the **tomatoes and cucumbers with basil oil**

5 ripe plum tomatoes

1 large cucumber

1 tablespoon basil oil or garlic-flavored olive oil

Salt and pepper to taste

1. Rinse the tomatoes, pat dry, and thinly slice. Peel and thinly slice the cucumber.

2. In a medium serving bowl, combine the tomato and cucumber slices, add the oil, and season with salt and pepper. Toss to coat. Place the bowl on the table with 4 small salad bowls or plates.

step 3

assemble the **peanut butter chocolate chip cookies**

8 oversize chocolate chip cookies

1/4 cup smooth or chunky peanut butter

Milk for serving (optional)

Spread the underside of 4 of the cookies with some of the peanut butter, then top each with a remaining cookie, top side up. Place on a serving plate.

step 4

serve

1. Add the reserved dressing to the arugula and toss to coat. Divide the arugula evenly among 4 dinner plates. Mound corn and bean salad in the center of each plate. Serve with the tomato and cucumber salad.

2. When ready for dessert, serve the cookies, with milk, if desired.

Corn and Black Bean Salad on Arugula
Single serving is 1/4 of the total recipe
CALORIES 318; PROTEIN 12g; CARBS 55g; TOTAL FAT 12g; SAT FAT 2g; CHOLESTEROL 0mg; SODIUM 887mg; FIBER 7g

four-bean salad
homemade bagel pizzas
fruit salad with toasted coconut

menu
gameplan

shopping list

Green beans

Red kidney beans

Black beans

Chickpeas

Red onion

Fresh parsley

Bagels

Pizza sauce

Pre-shredded part-skim mozzarella

Shredded coconut

Fruit salad
(fresh or jarred, from the produce department)

from your pantry

Cider vinegar

Canola oil

Sugar

Salt and pepper

serves 4

beforeyoustart
Preheat the oven to 450°F to toast the bagel pizzas.

| step | 1 | make the **four-bean salad** |

| step | 2 | prepare the **homemade bagel pizzas** |

| step | 3 | while the **bagels** are baking, prepare the **fruit salad** |

| step | 4 | **serve** |

 This salad becomes more flavorful as it stands. If possible, combine it ahead of time in a resealable plastic food storage bag. Store it in the refrigerator, turning it every now and then, to distribute the dressing. You'll be saving valuable time: There's no need to stir and less cleanup, too.

"The fresh green beans add color and crunch to this protein-filled salad. Fresh wax beans would be another good choice."

—minutemeals' Chef Hillary

step 1

make the **four-bean salad**

8 ounces green beans

Salt to taste

1 can (16 ounces) red kidney beans

1 can (16 ounces) black beans

1 can (16 ounces) chickpeas

1 small red onion

2 tablespoons chopped fresh parsley

1/2 cup cider vinegar

2 tablespoons canola oil

1 tablespoon sugar

Salt and pepper to taste

1. Trim the ends of the green beans, then cut into thirds. Fill a large skillet with 1/2 inch of water and bring to a boil, covered, over high heat. Add salt to taste and the green beans and cook for 3 to 4 minutes, until crisp-tender. Drain and rinse under cold running water.

2. Rinse and drain the red kidney beans, black beans, and chickpeas. Finely chop the red onion. Chop enough parsley to measure 2 tablespoons.

3. In a large salad bowl, with a fork, mix the vinegar, oil, and sugar until the sugar has dissolved. Season with salt and pepper.

4. Add the kidney beans, black beans, chickpeas, onion, parsley, and the cooked green beans. Toss gently to combine. Place the salad bowl on the table.

step 2

prepare the **homemade bagel pizzas**

4 plain bagels

1 cup (8 ounces) store-bought pizza sauce

8 ounces pre-shredded part-skim mozzarella

1. Preheat the oven to 450°F.

2. Split each bagel in half. Place the bagels, cut sides up, on a baking sheet and toast until lightly colored, about 3 minutes.

3. Spread each bagel half with pizza sauce and sprinkle with mozzarella. Bake for 5 minutes, or until the cheese is melted and bubbly. Transfer to a serving plate.

step 3

while the **bagels** are baking, prepare the **fruit salad with toasted coconut**

1/4 cup shredded coconut, or more to taste

Fresh fruit salad or jarred and drained for 4

While the pizza bagels are baking, spread the shredded coconut in a small baking pan and toast for 3 to 4 minutes, stirring once, until fragrant and golden brown. Remove.

step 4

serve

1. Serve the bean salad on 4 dinner plates and accompany with the bagel pizzas.

2. When ready for dessert, spoon the fruit salad into 4 dessert bowls and garnish each with a dusting of the toasted coconut. Serve.

Four-Bean Salad
Single serving is 1/4 of the total recipe
CALORIES 424; PROTEIN 23g; CARBS 66g;
TOTAL FAT 8g; SAT FAT 1g; CHOLESTEROL 0mg;
SODIUM 282mg; FIBER 17g

lentil salad
with goat cheese, olives, and oranges

herbed garlic yogurt dip with pita bread

easy strawberry shortcakes

menu
gameplan

serves 4

step 1 make the **salad**

step 2 make the **herbed garlic yogurt dip**

step 3 prepare the **easy strawberry shortcakes**

step 4 **serve**

shopping list

Canned lentils

Canned mandarin orange segments

Red onion

Fresh parsley

Ripe olives, pitted

Lemons (for juice)

Goat cheese

Lettuce leaves
(from the salad bar)

Plain low-fat yogurt

Scallion

Chives

Fresh mint

Pita bread

Ripe strawberries

Buttermilk biscuits
or blueberry muffins

Instant whipped cream,
light or regular

from your pantry

Garlic

Extra virgin olive oil

Ground cumin

Salt and pepper

Sugar

headsup

For a creamier yogurt dip, with cheese-like consistency, drain the yogurt, covered, in a colander set over a bowl in your refrigerator overnight. If you find yourself with no time at all to make dip, hummus makes a good stand-in.

"This salad is ideal when you want something a little more substantial than green salad but not quite as filling as pasta salad."

—minutemeals' Chef Hillary

step 1

make the **lentil salad with goat cheese, olives, and oranges**

2 cans (15 ounces each) lentils

1 can (11 ounces) mandarin orange segments

1 small red onion

1/2 cup chopped fresh parsley

1/2 cup chopped pitted ripe olives

2 garlic cloves

1/3 cup extra virgin olive oil

2 to 3 tablespoons fresh lemon juice (1 or 2 lemons)

1/2 to 1 teaspoon ground cumin

1 teaspoon salt

Freshly ground black pepper to taste

1 log (8 ounces) goat cheese

4 lettuce leaf cups for serving

1. Rinse and drain the lentils. Drain the mandarin oranges. Mince the red onion. Chop enough parsley to measure 1/2 cup. Chop enough olives to measure 1/2 cup.

2. Finely chop the garlic cloves. In a medium bowl, combine the garlic, olive oil, lemon juice to taste, cumin to taste, salt, and pepper until well blended.

3. Gently fold in the lentils, oranges, red onion, parsley, and olives and combine well.

4. Slice the goat cheese into 1/2-inch-thick rounds.

step 2

make the **herbed garlic yogurt dip**

1 pint plain low-fat yogurt

1 scallion

1 garlic clove

2 tablespoons snipped chives

1 tablespoon finely chopped fresh mint

4 pita breads

1. Drain the yogurt in a fine-mesh sieve lined with dampened cheesecloth or paper towels for 5 minutes.

2. Meanwhile, finely chop the scallion and garlic. Snip enough chives to measure 2 tablespoons. Finely chop enough mint to measure 1 tablespoon. Combine all in a medium bowl.

3. Add the drained yogurt and blend well. Transfer the dip to a wide shallow bowl and place in the middle of a serving platter.

4. Cut the pita breads into triangles and arrange around the edge of the platter. Place the platter on the table.

step 3

prepare the **easy strawberry shortcakes**

1 pint ripe strawberries

Sugar to taste

4 store-bought buttermilk biscuits or blueberry muffins

Instant whipped cream, light or regular

Rinse, hull, and quarter the strawberries into a bowl. Sprinkle with sugar to taste and toss. Let stand at room temperature until serving time.

step 4

serve

1. Place 1 lettuce leaf on each serving plate. Spoon lentil salad into and around each leaf and top each serving with 2 rounds of the goat cheese.

2. When ready for dessert, split each buttermilk biscuit or muffin in half horizontally and place on a dessert plate. Spoon some of the strawberries and juice over the bottom half of each biscuit or over both halves of the muffins. Garnish with whipped cream to taste and add the biscuit top. Serve. If desired, pass any remaining strawberries and additional whipped cream at the table.

Lentil Salad with Goat Cheese, Olives, and Oranges
Single serving is 1/4 of the total recipe
CALORIES 631; PROTEIN 31g; CARBS 54g;
TOTAL FAT 34g; SAT FAT 8g; CHOLESTEROL 26mg;
SODIUM 916mg; FIBER 19g

asian noodle and many vegetable salad

vegetable sushi

fresh pineapple parfaits

menu
gameplan

shopping list

Ramen noodles

Shredded red cabbage
(bagged, from the produce
department)

Fresh mung bean sprouts
or canned bean sprouts

Vegetable sushi (from the
specialty foods section or
the salad bar)

Wasabi paste (optional)

Pineapple ice or
vanilla ice cream

Sliced almonds (optional)

from the salad bar

Snow peas

Shredded carrots (or from the
produce department)

Celery slices

Chopped scallions

Cut-up fresh pineapple
chunks (or from the produce
department)

from your pantry

Salt

Lite soy sauce

Rice vinegar

Toasted sesame oil

Sugar

Ground ginger

Sesame seeds

serves 4

beforeyoustart

Bring a large pot of salted water to
a boil, covered, over high heat.
Remove the pineapple ice from the
freezer to soften.

step **1** make the **asian noodle and many vegetable salad**

step **2** plate the **vegetable sushi**

step **3** assemble the **fresh pineapple parfaits**

step **4** **serve**

 Vegetable sushi is more and
more available in supermar-
kets. If your market doesn't stock it, serve vegetable egg
rolls. Look for them in the international frozen foods case
and put them on to heat *before* making the salad.

"Mention Asian noodle salad and sesame noodles with creamy peanut sauce come to mind. This Asian noodle salad is totally different, and it's also delicious."

—minutemeals' Chef Hillary

step 1

make the **asian noodle and many vegetable salad**

For the noodles

3 quarts water

Salt to taste

2 cups snow peas

2 packages (5 ounce each) ramen noodles (discard the flavor packets)

For the salad

2 cups shredded red cabbage

2 cups shredded carrots

1 cup celery slices

1 cup fresh mung bean sprouts or 1 can (8 ounces) bean sprouts

1/2 cup chopped scallions

1/3 cup lite soy sauce

1/3 cup rice vinegar

4 teaspoons toasted sesame oil

1 teaspoon sugar

1/2 teaspoon ground ginger

1 tablespoon sesame seeds

1. Cook the noodles: Pour the water into a large pot, salt lightly, and cover. Bring to a boil over high heat.

2. While the water is coming to a boil, trim and string the snow peas.

3. When the water is at a rolling boil, add the ramen noodles, stirring to separate, and the snow peas and cook for 3 minutes. Drain in a colander and rinse under cold water to stop the cooking.

4. Make the salad: In a large, preferably shallow, salad bowl, combine the cabbage, carrots, celery, bean sprouts (if using canned sprouts, drain and rinse before using), and scallions, and toss to mix. Add the ramen noodles and snow peas and toss until combined.

5. In a bowl, with a fork, stir together the soy sauce, vinegar, sesame oil, sugar, and ginger until the sugar is dissolved. Pour the dressing over the salad and toss until coated. Sprinkle with the sesame seeds.

step 2

plate the **vegetable sushi**

20 pieces vegetable sushi

Lite soy sauce for serving

Wasabi paste for serving (optional)

Arrange the vegetable sushi on a serving platter and place on the table with small serving plates. Accompany with soy sauce for dipping and wasabi paste, if desired.

step 3

assemble the **fresh pineapple parfaits**

Cut-up fresh pineapple chunks for 4

1 pint pineapple ice or vanilla ice cream, softened

Sliced almonds (optional)

1. Cut the pineapple chunks into smaller pieces.

2. Scoop softened pineapple ice or vanilla ice cream into 4 parfait or wine glasses. Top with some of the cut-up pineapple. Continue to make layers with the remaining ingredients, ending with a topping of fresh pineapple. Place the parfaits in the freezer until serving time.

step 4

serve

1. Serve the noodle salad on 4 large dinner plates accompanied by the vegetable sushi.

2. When ready for dessert, garnish each parfait with sliced almonds, if desired. Serve.

Asian Noodle and Many Vegetable Salad
Single serving is 1/4 of the total recipe

CALORIES 376; PROTEIN 20g; CARBS 58g; TOTAL FAT 7g; SAT FAT 1g; CHOLESTEROL 0mg; SODIUM 789mg; FIBER 17g

pizza pasta salad
strawberries with pound cake

shopping list

Shaped pasta, such as shells
or penne

Fresh basil

Presliced mushrooms
(from the produce department)

Pre-shredded part-skim
mozzarella

Strawberries

Pound cake

Instant whipped cream
or topping (optional)

from the salad bar

Cherry tomatoes

Green pepper strips

from your pantry

Garlic

Olive oil

Cider vinegar

Dried oregano

Salt and freshly ground
black pepper

Grated Parmesan cheese
(optional)

Confectioners' sugar

Grand Marnier
(or orange juice)

serves 4

beforeyoustart

Bring the water to a boil in a large
pot, covered, over high heat to cook
the pasta.

| step | 1 | make the **pizza pasta salad** |

| step | 2 | prepare the **strawberries with pound cake** |

| step | 3 | **serve** |

 If you want to make the salad
ahead of time, keep it covered
in the refrigerator for safety reasons. And because pasta
absorbs liquid as it stands, you may need to add more oil
and vinegar before serving. A little more fresh basil would
perk it up, too. Do not add the Parmesan: It will clump.

step 1

make the **pizza pasta salad**

- 4 quarts water
- Salt, to taste
- 12 ounces shaped pasta, such as shells or penne
- 1 pint cherry tomatoes
- 1 cup green pepper slices
- 1/2 cup chopped fresh basil
- 2 or 3 garlic cloves
- 1/3 cup olive oil
- 1/4 cup cider vinegar
- 1 teaspoon dried oregano
- 1 box (8 ounces) sliced mushrooms
- 1 cup pre-shredded part-skim mozzarella cheese
- Salt and freshly ground black pepper to taste
- Grated Parmesan cheese for serving (optional)

1. Cook the pasta: Pour the water into a pasta pot, salt the water lightly, and cover the pot. Bring the water to a boil over high heat. Add the pasta and cook according to the directions on the package. Drain. Rinse under cold water and drain well again.

2. While the pasta is cooking, rinse the cherry tomatoes, pat dry, and halve. Chop the green pepper and enough fresh basil to measure 1/2 cup. Finely chop the garlic. Place all in a large bowl.

3. Add the olive oil, cider vinegar, oregano, sliced mushrooms, and mozzarella and toss to combine. Season generously with salt and pepper.

4. Add the cooked pasta and toss well. Taste and correct the seasonings.

step 2

prepare the **strawberries with pound cake**

- 2 pints strawberries
- 3 tablespoons confectioners' sugar
- 1 tablespoon Grand Marnier or orange juice
- Store-bought pound cake
- Instant whipped cream or topping (optional)

Rinse, hull, and quarter the strawberries. In a bowl, combine the strawberries with the confectioners' sugar and Grand Marnier or orange juice. Toss gently. Let stand until serving time.

step 3

serve

1. Divide the pasta salad evenly among 4 pasta bowls and serve, with a bowl of Parmesan cheese for sprinkling on top, if desired.

2. When ready to serve dessert, cut the pound cake into four 1/2-inch-thick slices. Place 1 slice on each of 4 dessert plates. Spoon strawberries with their juices over the top of each slice and garnish with whipped cream, if desired. Serve.

Pizza Pasta Salad
Single serving is 1/4 of the total recipe
CALORIES 445; PROTEIN 19g; CARBS 32g;
TOTAL FAT 27g; SAT FAT 7g; CHOLESTEROL 23mg;
SODIUM 236mg; FIBER 3g

couscous-and-vegetable-stuffed bell peppers

cucumbers and grape tomatoes with hummus

marble pound cake with kahlúa chocolate sauce

shopping list

Plain couscous

Firm red peppers

Zucchini

Fresh parsley or cilantro

Chickpeas

Chopped scallions
(from the salad bar)

Cucumbers

Grape tomatoes

Hummus, plain or flavored

Marble pound cake

Instant whipped cream
(optional)

from your pantry

Vegetable broth

Olive oil

Rice vinegar

Ground cumin

Salt and pepper

Chocolate sauce

Kahlúa (coffee-flavored
liqueur)

serves 6

step **1** prepare the **stuffed bell peppers**

step **2** prepare the **cucumbers and grape tomatoes**

step **3** prepare the **marble pound cake**

step **4** **serve**

 Bell peppers, or sweet peppers, are extremely healthful. Red bell peppers are high in Vitamin C, more so than green bell peppers. Peppers used for stuffing should be firm.

"These peppers are pretty and delicious. There are easy ways to vary the filling. Add dried cherries or peas. Or substitute rice for the couscous."

—minutemeals' Chef Hillary

step 1

prepare the **couscous-and-vegetable-stuffed bell peppers**

For the couscous

2 cups vegetable broth or water

1 tablespoon olive oil

1 box (9 ounces) plain couscous

For the vegetables

6 firm medium red peppers

1 medium zucchini

1/2 cup chopped fresh parsley or cilantro

1 can (16 ounces) chickpeas

1/2 cup chopped scallions

1/4 cup rice vinegar

2 teaspoons ground cumin

2 tablespoons olive oil

Salt and pepper to taste

1. Prepare the couscous: Put the vegetable broth or water and olive oil in a 2-quart saucepan, cover, and bring to a boil over high heat. Stir in the couscous. Cover and remove the pan from the heat. Let stand for 5 minutes. Fluff the couscous with a fork, transfer it to a large mixing bowl, and let cool.

2. Prepare the vegetables: Rinse the peppers, pat dry, and cut off the tops, reserving them. Core and seed the peppers. Trim the base of each pepper slightly so that it has a flat surface. Chop the tops and bottoms of the peppers and add to the couscous.

3. Trim the ends off the zucchini, and coarsely chop. Chop enough parsley or cilantro to measure 1/2 cup. Rinse and drain the chickpeas.

4. Add the zucchini, parsley, chickpeas, scallions, vinegar, cumin, olive oil, salt and pepper to the couscous. Toss well to combine and spoon into the pepper shells.

step 2

prepare the **cucumbers and grape tomatoes with hummus**

2 large cucumbers

1 pint grape tomatoes

1 container (8 ounces) plain or flavored hummus

1. Peel the cucumbers, cut into quarters lengthwise, and cut away the seeds in each section. Cut the quarters into thinner spears. Place around the rim of a serving platter.

2. Rinse the grape tomatoes and pat dry. Add to the platter. Place the platter on the table with the hummus.

step 3

prepare the **marble pound cake with kahlúa chocolate sauce**

1 store-bought marble pound cake

1 jar good-quality chocolate sauce

2 tablespoons Kahlúa

Instant whipped cream (optional)

1. Preheat the broiler or a large toaster oven. Line a jelly-roll pan with aluminum foil.

2. Cut the pound cake into 6 even slices and arrange in one layer on the pan. Broil for 30 seconds to 1 minute per side, or until lightly toasted.

step 4

serve

1. Place a stuffed pepper on each dinner plate and serve with the cucumber and tomatoes with hummus.

2. When ready for dessert, warm the chocolate sauce in the microwave oven according to the directions on the jar until hot. Transfer to a heat-proof bowl and stir in the Kahlúa. Spoon some of the chocolate sauce over each slice of pound cake and garnish with whipped cream, if desired. Serve with the remaining chocolate sauce.

Couscous-and-Vegetable-Stuffed Bell Peppers
Single serving is 1/6 of the total recipe
CALORIES 273; PROTEIN 9g; CARBS 41g;
TOTAL FAT 8g; SAT FAT 1g; CHOLESTEROL 0mg;
SODIUM 362mg; FIBER 4g

panzanella with gorgonzola
(italian bread salad with tomatoes and cheese)
mixed olives
fresh figs with port wine

serves 6

shopping list

Fresh figs

Orange (for zest)

Port wine

Tuscan-style bread

Tomatoes

Celery

Red onion

Jarred roasted red peppers

Capers

Basil leaves

Gorgonzola cheese

Mixed olives, such as niçoise, kalamata, or Gaeta

from your pantry

Sugar

Garlic

Extra virgin olive oil

Salt and pepper

step	1	prepare the **fresh figs with port wine**
step	2	assemble the **panzanella with gorgonzola**
step	3	plate the **mixed olives**
step	4	**serve**

headsup
Here's a way to make removing the zest from a piece of citrus fruit less challenging: Place a piece of plastic wrap directly on the surface of a hand-held box grater, pressing it on so that the grates come through. Grate the fruit with the wrap in place. When you're done, lift the plastic wrap off and scrape the zest off the wrap. It makes cleanup easier, too.

"I am amazed at the quality of bread now available at the supermarket. If you can't find a Tuscan-style bread use sourdough bread for this salad."

—minutemeals' Chef Hillary

step 1

prepare the **fresh figs with port wine**

12 fresh figs

1 teaspoon grated orange zest (1 orange)

1/4 cup port wine

2 tablespoons sugar

1. Rinse the figs and remove the stem on each. Cut the figs in half through the stem ends. Place in a medium bowl.

2. Grate enough orange to measure 1 teaspoon zest. Add the zest to the figs with the port and sugar and toss gently to combine. Let stand at room temperature while you make the salad.

step 2

assemble the **panzanella with gorgonzola**

8 ounces crusty Tuscan-style bread

6 large tomatoes

2 large garlic cloves, or more to taste

4 stalks celery from the heart

1 medium red onion

1 jar (12 ounces) roasted red peppers

2 tablespoons drained capers

1/2 cup chopped fresh basil leaves

1/2 cup extra virgin olive oil

4 to 6 ounces crumbled Gorgonzola cheese

Salt and pepper to taste

1. Tear the bread into bite-sized pieces and place in a large salad bowl. Core the tomatoes and cut them into large chunks. Add them to the bowl and toss with the bread. Set the bowl aside.

2. Mince the garlic. Chop the celery and red onion. Drain and chop the roasted peppers. Add all to the salad bowl along with the capers.

3. Chop enough basil leaves to measure 1/2 cup. Add the basil to the bowl with the olive oil and Gorgonzola. Toss gently to combine, season with salt and pepper, and toss again.

step 3

plate the **mixed olives**

8 ounces mixed olives, such as niçoise, kalamata, or Gaeta

Put the olives in a shallow serving bowl.

step 4

serve

1. At serving time, bring the bread salad and bowl of olives to the table.

2. When ready to serve dessert, place 4 fig halves in each of 4 small bowls. Spoon some of the juices over each portion. Serve.

Panzanella with Gorgonzola
Single serving is 1/6 of the total recipe
CALORIES 346; PROTEIN 8g; CARBS 31g;
TOTAL FAT 23g; SAT FAT 4g; CHOLESTEROL 9mg;
SODIUM 568mg; FIBER 7g

exotic fruit salad
with ginger and mint

garlicky cheese spread
with pita triangles

vegetable platter
with hummus

shortbread

shopping list

Gingerroot
Limes
Mangoes
Kiwis
Strawberries
Canned pineapple chunks, packed in juice
Mint leaves
Nonfat vanilla yogurt
Whole-wheat pita pockets
Fresh parsley
Low-fat cottage cheese
Hummus
Assorted olives (from the olive bar or jarred)
Shortbread

from the salad bar

Tomato wedges
Cucumber spears

from your pantry

Honey
Garlic
Dried thyme
Dried basil
Dried oregano
Salt and pepper

serves 4

beforeyoustart

Preheat the oven to 400° to heat the pita pockets.

step 1 prepare the **exotic fruit salad with ginger and mint**

step 2 prepare the **cheese spread with pita triangles**

step 3 plate the **vegetable platter with hummus**

step 4 serve

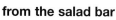 Color is not always a sign of a mango's ripeness, but aroma is and so is a certain give to the flesh when pressed. To ripen a mango place it in a paper bag with an apple and seal the bag tight. Let stand on the counter for a few days until fragrant and slightly softened.

step 1

prepare the **exotic fruit salad with ginger and mint**

For the dressing

1 one-inch piece ginger

1/4 cup honey

Juice of 2 limes

The fruits

2 medium mangoes

4 ripe kiwis

2 cups strawberries

1 can (20 ounces) pineapple chunks in their own juice

1/2 cup mint leaves

2 cups nonfat vanilla yogurt

1. Make the dressing: Peel and grate the ginger. Place in a medium-large bowl. Add the honey and lime juice and stir with a fork until combined.

2. Prepare the fruits: Peel the mangoes. With a sharp knife, slice the fruit off the pits and cut into 1-inch chunks. Peel the kiwis and quarter them. Rinse, hull, and quarter the strawberries. Drain the pineapple. Measure 1/2 cup loosely packed mint leaves; rinse and pat dry.

3. Add all the fruit to the dressing. Tear the mint leaves into medium pieces and add to the salad. Toss gently to combine. Let stand at room temperature until ready to serve.

step 2

prepare the **garlicky cheese spread with pita triangles**

4 whole-wheat pita pockets

1 garlic clove

1 tablespoon chopped fresh parsley

1 pint low-fat cottage cheese

1 teaspoon dried thyme

1/2 teaspoon dried basil

1/4 teaspoon dried oregano

1. Preheat the oven to 400°F. Stack the pita pockets and wrap the stack in aluminum foil. Heat for 3 to 5 minutes, until warm through. Remove, but do not unwrap.

2. Make the cottage cheese spread: Crush the garlic with the flat side of a large knife. Chop enough parsley to measure 1 tablespoon.

3. In a food processor or blender, combine the garlic, parsley, cottage cheese, thyme, basil, and oregano. Process for 1 minute, or until smooth. Scrape the mixture into a serving bowl.

step 3

plate the **vegetable platter with hummus**

Tomato wedges for 4

Cucumber spears for 4

1 container (8 ounces) prepared hummus

Assorted olives

Arrange the tomatoes and cucumbers around the edge of a serving platter. Place the hummus in the center. Serve the olives in a small bowl with the platter. Place the platter and olives on the table with 4 salad plates.

step 4

serve

1. Divide the fruit salad among 4 salad bowls. Top each salad with 1/2 cup of the vanilla yogurt and serve.

2. Cut the pita pockets into wedges, place in a basket, and serve with the cottage cheese spread and hummus and vegetable platter.

3. When ready for dessert, cut the shortbread into wedges and serve on a plate.

Exotic Fruit Salad with Ginger and Mint
Single serving is 1/4 of the total recipe
CALORIES 302; PROTEIN 9g; CARBS 71g; FAT 2g; SAT FAT 0g; CHOLESTEROL 1mg; SODIUM 100mg; FIBER 7g

herbed vegetable salad

warm goat cheese croustades

berry compote with crème de cassis

menu
gameplan

shopping list

Fresh herbs, such as parsley and chives

Goat cheese

French bread

Blackberries or blueberries

Raspberries

Crème de cassis (black currant liqueur)

Sugar wafers (optional)

Chickpeas

Jarred roasted red peppers

Prewashed Italian-style salad mix or mixed greens from the salad bar

from the salad bar

Broccoli florets

Sliced red onion or sweet white onion

from your pantry

Garlic

Olive oil

White wine vinegar

Sugar

Salt and pepper

serves 4

beforeyoustart

Preheat the broiler to make the goat cheese croustades.

step 1 prepare the **warm goat cheese croustades**

step 2 prepare the **berry compote with crème de cassis**

step 3 assemble the **herbed vegetable salad**

step 4 **serve**

luckyforyou

There are a lot of different varieties of soft goat cheeses available in the supermarket. Some are already marinated in herbed oil. Buy one of those and you'll be saving yourself a good bit of prep time.

make the **kaleidoscope potato salad**

> 1 pound small, cut-up red potatoes, 1/2-inch chunks
>
> 1 cup red pepper slices
>
> 1/4 cup olive oil
>
> 1/4 cup cider vinegar
>
> Salt and pepper to taste
>
> 1/2 cup chopped scallions
>
> 2 tablespoons snipped fresh dill

1. Put the cut-up potatoes in a 2-quart saucepan, add cold water to cover, and salt lightly. Cover and bring to a boil over high heat. Reduce the heat to medium and simmer for 7 to 10 minutes, or until the potatoes are just tender. Drain and immediately add to the dressing.

2. While the potatoes are cooking, make the dressing. Coarsely chop the red pepper slices.

3. In a medium bowl, with a fork, whisk together the olive oil and vinegar. Season with salt and pepper. Stir in the scallions and chopped red pepper and blend well.

4. Add the warm potatoes to the dressing and toss to coat.

5. Snip enough dill to measure 2 tablespoons; reserve.

cook the **veggie burgers on whole-wheat buns**

> 4 whole-wheat hamburger buns
>
> 4 veggie burgers
>
> 1 large tomato
>
> 1 medium red onion
>
> Lettuce leaves
>
> Ketchup and/or mustard

1. Preheat the broiler (or a large toaster oven). Split each bun in half. Arrange the buns on the broiler pan and toast for 1 to 2 minutes, or until golden.

2. Cook the veggie burgers according to the directions on the package.

3. While the burgers are cooking, rinse the tomato, pat dry, and thinly slice. Slice the red onion. Arrange onion and tomato slices and lettuce leaves on a small platter.

prepare the **hot fudge sundaes**

> Your favorite ice cream
>
> Jarred fudge sauce
>
> Chopped nuts, such as walnuts, almonds, or hazelnuts
>
> Instant light whipped cream (optional)

1. Remove the ice cream from the freezer to soften.

2. Warm the fudge sauce in the microwave oven according to the directions on the jar.

serve

1. Sprinkle the potato salad with the reserved dill and toss to combine.

2. Place a veggie burger on the bottom half of each hamburger bun and place on a plate. Serve open faced or top with the remaining buns with the sliced red onion, tomatoes, ketchup, and mustard.

3. When ready for dessert, scoop ice cream into 4 dessert bowls and top generously with hot fudge sauce. Sprinkle with chopped nuts, add whipped cream, if desired, and serve.

Kaleidoscope Potato Salad
Single serving is 1/4 of the total recipe
CALORIES 195; PROTEIN 2g; CARBS 17g;
TOTAL FAT 14g; SAT FAT 0g; CHOLESTEROL 0mg;
SODIUM 5mg; FIBER 2g

spinach salad
with black beans and mandarin oranges
deviled eggs
brownies à la mode

menu gameplan

shopping list

Peeled hard-cooked eggs (from the salad bar)

Low-fat plain yogurt or reduced-fat sour cream

Slivered almonds

Black beans

Canned mandarin oranges

Red onion

Prewashed baby spinach leaves

Brownies

Vanilla ice cream

from your pantry

Reduced-fat mayonnaise

Dijon mustard

Dried dill weed

Red or green Tabasco sauce

Salt and freshly ground black pepper

Paprika

Vegetable oil

Red wine vinegar

Sugar

serves 4

step **1** make the **deviled eggs**

step **2** assemble the **spinach salad**

step **3** prepare the **brownies à la mode**

step **4** **serve**

luckyforyou Baby spinach leaves are available bagged in most supermarkets. It is ready to use. If it isn't available where you shop, look for bagged larger-leafed spinach that is labeled "prewashed." Fresh spinach in bunches is notoriously sandy, and not an option here.

"For the deviled eggs, mound the filling into the whites with a baby spoon. It is easier to control and, therefore, saves time." —minutemeals' Chef Hillary

make the **deviled eggs**

8 peeled hard-cooked eggs

1 tablespoon reduced-fat mayonnaise

1 tablespoon low-fat plain yogurt or reduced-fat sour cream

1 teaspoon Dijon mustard

1 teaspoon dried dill weed

Red or green Tabasco sauce to taste

Salt and pepper to taste

Paprika for serving

1. Cut each of the eggs in half. Scoop out the yolk, reserving the white. Put the yolks in a medium bowl. Add the mayonnaise, yogurt, mustard, dill, Tabasco, and salt and pepper. Mash well with a fork until smooth.

2. Spoon the yolk mixture into the egg whites, mounding it on top, and sprinkle paprika over all. Place the eggs on a serving platter and refrigerate until serving time.

assemble the **spinach salad with black beans and mandarin oranges**

3 tablespoons vegetable oil

1/2 cup slivered almonds

2 tablespoons red wine vinegar

2 teaspoons sugar

1/4 teaspoon salt

1/8 teaspoon freshly ground black pepper

1 can (16 ounces) black beans

1 can (11 ounces) mandarin oranges

1 small red onion

2 bags (5 to 6 ounces each) prewashed baby spinach leaves

1. In a large skillet, heat the oil over medium heat. Add the almonds and cook, stirring, until golden, 2 to 3 minutes. Remove the skillet from the heat and using a slotted spoon transfer the almonds to a plate and reserve.

2. To the oil in the skillet add the vinegar, sugar, salt, and pepper. Stir until the sugar is dissolved. Remove the pan from the heat.

3. Rinse and drain the beans. Drain the oranges. Thinly slice the red onion.

4. In a large salad bowl, combine the spinach, beans, oranges, and red onion. Pour the dressing over the salad and toss well. Sprinkle the toasted almonds over the top. Place the salad on the table.

prepare the **brownies à la mode**

4 store-bought brownies

Vanilla ice cream

1. Place each brownie on a dessert plate.

2. Remove the ice cream from the freezer to soften while having dinner.

serve

1. Serve the spinach salad at the table accompanied by the deviled eggs.

2. When ready for dessert, scoop vanilla ice cream onto each brownie. Serve.

Spinach Salad with Black Beans and Mandarin Oranges
Single serving is 1/4 of the total recipe
(includes 2 deviled egg halves per serving)
CALORIES 472; PROTEIN 23g; CARBS 35g; TOTAL FAT 28g; SAT FAT 5g; CHOLESTEROL 431mg; SODIUM 751mg; FIBER 9g

fried green tomato stack salad

corn on the cob with cumin-shallot butter

raspberries and pound cake with whipped cream

menu gameplan

shopping list

Green or firm pink tomatoes

Pre-shredded smoked mozzarella

Prewashed baby salad greens

Corn on the cob

Shallot

Pound cake (from the bakery)

Raspberries

Instant whipped cream

from your pantry

Yellow cornmeal

Salt and pepper

Olive oil

Quality vinaigrette, store-bought

Butter

Ground cumin

serves 4

step	**1**	make the **fried green tomato stack salad**
step	**2**	microwave the **corn on the cob with cumin-shallot butter**
step	**3**	**serve**

 Shallots, part of the onion family, are now sold in supermarkets in small packages, sometimes containing as few as 3. It wasn't too long ago that buying shallots meant having to buy a lot of them. If you don't have shallots or can't buy just 1, use a heaping tablespoon of chopped red onion, Vidalia onion, or even chopped scallion green.

"Corn on the cob can also be microwaved right in its husks. Microwave for the time recommended by your microwave manufacturer."

—minutemeals' Chef Miriam

step 1

make the **fried green tomato stack salad**

- 3 green or firm pink (partly ripe) tomatoes (about 1 pound)
- 1/3 cup yellow cornmeal
- 1/4 teaspoon salt
- 1/4 teaspoon pepper
- 3 tablespoons olive oil
- 1 cup pre-shredded smoked mozzarella
- 1 package (5 ounces) prewashed baby salad greens
- 1/3 cup quality store-bought vinaigrette

1. Trim off ends of the tomatoes and slice into twelve 1/4-inch-thick slices.

2. Combine the cornmeal and salt and pepper in a pie plate. Dip the tomatoes into cornmeal mixture, pressing it on the surface, and place on a sheet of waxed paper.

3. Divide the oil between 2 large nonstick skillets and heat over medium heat until hot but not smoking. Add the tomato slices in a single layer to each skillet and fry for 3 minutes. With a metal spatula, turn the tomatoes and sprinkle a rounded tablespoon of the cheese over each slice. Cook for 2 to 3 minutes more.

4. Remove the tomato slices from the skillets. Let cool slightly, then make 4 stacks of 3 slices each

step 2

microwave the **corn on the cob with cumin-shallot butter**

- 4 ears shucked corn on the cob
- 1 shallot
- 3 tablespoons butter
- 1/4 teaspoon ground cumin
- 1/4 teaspoon each salt and pepper

1. Place the ears of corn in a microwave-safe dish. Add 1/4 cup water and cover with vented plastic wrap. Microwave on High for 6 to 8 minutes, or just until tender.

2. Meanwhile, chop the shallot and place in a small microwave-safe dish. Add the butter and cumin, cover with vented plastic wrap, and microwave on High for 1 minute, or until the butter is melted and the shallot is tender.

step 3

serve

1. Cover each of 4 dinner plates with salad greens. Set a stack of the fried tomatoes in the center, then drizzle each serving with some of the vinaigrette. Serve.

2. Drain the corn, place it on a platter, and place the platter and flavored butter on the table.

3. When ready for dessert, cut the pound cake into 4 slices and place on 4 dessert plates. Top each with raspberries and whipped cream. Serve, with additional whipped cream, if desired.

Fried Green Tomato Stack Salad
Single serving is 1/4 of the total recipe
CALORIES 301; PROTEIN 9g; CARBS 15g; TOTAL FAT 24g; SAT FAT 5g; CHOLESTEROL 22mg; SODIUM 408mg; FIBER 2g

vegetable salad niçoise

whole-grain rolls with olive oil
latticetop berry tart

shopping list

Prewashed salad greens

Dijon vinaigrette

Swiss cheese, sliced

Whole-grain rolls

Latticetop berry tart

from the salad bar

Peeled hard-cooked eggs

Red and green pepper slices

Mushrooms slices (or from the produce department)

Cooked green beans

Cherry tomatoes

Shredded carrots or cabbage (or from the produce department)

Cooked potatoes, sliced or cut in chunks

Cucumber slices

from your pantry

Salt and pepper

Extra virgin olive oil

serves 4

beforeyoustart

Preheat the oven to 400°F to heat the rolls.

step **1** assemble the **vegetable salad niçoise**

step **2** heat the **whole-grain rolls with olive oil**

step **3** **serve**

 Substitutions are the name of the game for this salad. Use what appeals to you: jarred beets, marinated mushrooms, chopped celery, and so on.

"An assertively flavored vinaigrette adds a lot to this salad. Or, if you're not a strict vegetarian, add anchovies, as they do in Nice."

—minutemeals' Chef Hillary

assemble the **vegetable salad niçoise**

1 bag (5 to 6 ounces) prewashed salad greens

1/3 cup store-bought Dijon vinaigrette

Salt and pepper to taste

4 ounces sliced Swiss cheese

4 peeled hard-cooked eggs

1 cup red and green pepper slices

1/2 cup mushroom slices

2 cups cooked green beans

2 cups cherry tomatoes

1 cup cooked potatoes, sliced or cut in chunks

1 cup cucumber slices

1/2 cup shredded carrots or cabbage

1. In a large bowl, toss the salad greens with 2 tablespoons of the Dijon vinaigrette and season with salt and pepper. Spread the dressed greens on a large platter.

2. Cut the Swiss cheese into thin strips. Quarter the hard-cooked eggs.

3. In the same bowl, combine the pepper slices, mushrooms, green beans, cherry tomatoes, potatoes, cucumbers, carrots, Swiss cheese, and remaining vinaigrette and toss to combine well. Season with salt and pepper. Mound the vegetable mixture on the greens. Arrange the hard-cooked egg quarters around the salad.

heat the **whole-grain rolls with olive oil**

4 to 6 whole-grain rolls

1/4 cup good quality extra virgin olive oil for dipping

1. Preheat the oven to 400°F.

2. Put the rolls directly on the oven rack and heat until just warm. Serve with good quality extra virgin olive oil.

serve

1. Serve the salad on large dinner plates accompanied by the warm rolls and olive oil for dipping.

2. When ready for dessert, cut the tart into slices and place on 4 dessert plates. Serve.

Vegetable Niçoise Salad
Single serving is 1/4 of the total recipe

CALORIES 280; PROTEIN 16g; CARBS 20g;
TOTAL FAT 15g; SAT FAT 5g; CHOLESTEROL 33mg;
SODIUM 395mg; FIBER 5g

mediterranean grilled vegetable salad

micro-baked potatoes with sour cream

honeydew melon with honey and lemon

menu gameplan

serves 4

shopping list

Thin-skinned potatoes

Light sour cream

Red or green peppers

Zucchini

Red onion

Diced tomatoes

White beans

Fresh mozzarella

Fresh basil or parsley

Balsamic vinaigrette

Precut honeydew melon (from the salad bar or produce department)

Lemons (for juice)

from your pantry

Olive oil cooking spray

Salt and pepper

Garlic

Honey

step **1** prepare the **micro-baked potatoes with sour cream**

step **2** make the **grilled vegetable salad**

step **3** prepare the **honeydew melon**

step **4** **serve**

If you love ratatouille, you probably love eggplant, an essential, if not *the* essential ingredient of ratatouille, when there's more than 20 minutes to make it! You can have eggplant in this minutemeal salad, though: Just stir a jar of caponata into the vegetables before serving.

"I like to use the broiler for that 'grilled' flavor on the peppers and zucchini, but a grill pan will work too."

—minutemeals' Chef Hillary

step 1

prepare the **micro-baked potatoes with sour cream**

1 pound thin-skinned potatoes

Light sour cream for serving

Scrub the potatoes and prick in several places with a fork. Place in the microwave oven and microwave on High for 4 to 7 minutes, turning 2 or 3 times, until tender. Remove from the microwave and wrap loosely in a clean towel. Let stand 5 minutes before serving.

step 2

make the **mediterranean grilled vegetable salad**

Olive oil cooking spray

2 red or green peppers

2 medium zucchini

Salt and pepper to taste

1 small red onion

1 medium garlic clove

1 can (14$\frac{1}{2}$ ounces) diced tomatoes

1 can (15 to 16 ounces) white beans

8 ounces fresh mozzarella

2 tablespoons chopped fresh basil or parsley

$\frac{1}{4}$ cup prepared balsamic vinaigrette

1. Preheat the broiler. Mist a jelly-roll pan with the olive oil spray.

2. Cut the peppers into $\frac{1}{2}$-inch pieces. Trim the zucchini and cut into $\frac{1}{2}$-inch pieces. Combine the peppers and zucchini on the jelly-roll pan, spray with olive oil spray, and season with salt and pepper. Broil 4 to 5 inches from the heat for 5 to 7 minutes, or until softened and starting to brown. Remove from the oven and transfer to a serving bowl.

3. While the peppers and zucchini are cooking, chop the red onion. Crush the garlic in a garlic press. Drain the tomatoes. Drain and rinse the beans. Chop the mozzarella into cubes. Chop enough basil or parsley to measure 2 tablespoons.

4. Add the red onion tomatoes, beans, mozzarella, garlic, basil, and vinaigrette to the vegetables and toss well until thoroughly combined. Season generously with salt and pepper.

step 3

prepare the **honeydew melon with honey and lemon**

Precut honeydew melon for 4

2 tablespoons honey

Juice of 2 lemons

In a medium bowl, combine the melon, honey, and lemon juice and toss gently to combine. Let stand at room temperature until serving time.

step 4

serve

1. Divide the salad among 4 dinner plates and serve.

2. Transfer the potatoes to a serving bowl and serve with sour cream as a topping.

3. When ready for dessert, divide the melon among 4 small dessert bowls, spoon any honeyed lemon juice in the bowl over the fruit, and serve.

Mediterranean Grilled Vegetable Salad
Single serving is $\frac{1}{4}$ of the total recipe
CALORIES 84.92; PROTEIN 2.85g; CARBS 15.77g; TOTAL FAT 1.55g; SAT FAT 0.30g; CHOLESTEROL 0mg; SODIUM 428.77mg; FIBER 4.50g

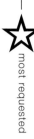
★ waldorf salad
with a twist (or two)
parmesan breadsticks
coffee caramel sundaes

menu gameplan

shopping list

Watercress

Havarti cheese

Granny Smith or other tart apples

Reduced-fat sour cream

Lemon (for juice)

Chopped walnuts

Plain breadsticks

Caramel sauce

Coffee sorbet

Mini semisweet chocolate morsels

from the salad bar

Celery sticks

Seedless red and/or green grapes

Chopped scallions

Peeled hard-cooked extra large eggs

from your pantry

Reduced-fat mayonnaise

Celery seeds (optional)

Salt

Olive oil

Grated Parmesan cheese

Coarsely ground black pepper

serves 4

step 1 assemble the **waldorf salad with a twist (or two)**

step 2 heat the **parmesan breadsticks**

step 3 prepare the **coffee caramel sundaes**

step 4 **serve**

luckyforyou
Even if you have run out of time to make your own breadsticks, you can still have hot breadsticks with this menu. Buy ready-to-bake garlic breadsticks in the refrigerator case and heat them while you make the salad.

"Havarti is a mild-flavored soft cheese. It contrasts beautifully with the crunchiness of the apples and walnuts in this healthful Waldorf salad."

—minutemeals' Chef Hillary

step 1

assemble the **waldorf salad with a twist (or two)**

2 bunches of watercress

6 ounces Havarti cheese

1 cup celery sticks

2 medium Granny Smith or other tart apples

2 cups seedless red or green grapes, or a combination of both

1/2 cup chopped scallions

3 tablespoons reduced-fat mayonnaise

3 tablespoons reduced-fat sour cream

Juice of 1 lemon

1/4 teaspoon celery seeds (optional)

Salt and pepper to taste

1/3 cup chopped walnuts

4 peeled hard-cooked extra large eggs

1. Remove the tough stems from the watercress, rinse the leaves and tender stems, and spin dry. Cut the Havarti into small pieces. Chop the celery to measure about 3/4 cup.

2. Core the apples, cut into 1/2-inch chunks, and place in a large bowl. Add the grapes, cheese, celery, and scallions.

3. Add the mayonnaise, sour cream, lemon juice, celery seeds, if using, and season generously with salt and pepper. Toss well to combine.

step 2

heat the **parmesan breadsticks**

8 plain breadsticks

2 teaspoons olive oil

2 tablespoons grated Parmesan cheese

1/4 teaspoon coarsely ground black pepper

1. Preheat the oven to 350°F.

2. Lay the breadsticks on a jelly-roll pan and brush with the olive oil.

3. In a small bowl, combine the Parmesan and black pepper. Sprinkle it evenly over the breadsticks. Bake for 2 to 3 minutes, or until the cheese has melted slightly and the breadsticks are warm.

step 3

prepare the **coffee caramel sundaes**

1 small jar caramel sauce

1 pint coffee sorbet

2 tablespoons mini semisweet chocolate morsels

1. Place the jar of caramel sauce in a small saucepan half filled with hot tap water and let stand until pourable. Or warm the sauce in the microwave oven according to the directions on the jar.

2. Remove the sorbet from the freezer to soften.

step 4

serve

1. Divide the watercress evenly among 4 dinner plates and mound the Waldorf salad in the middle. Sprinkle each serving with some of the chopped walnuts.

2. Quarter each hard-cooked egg and add 4 quarters to each salad. Serve at once with the warm breadsticks.

3. When ready for dessert, scoop the sorbet into 4 small dessert bowls and spoon some of the caramel sauce over the top. Sprinkle with the chocolate morsels and serve while the caramel sauce is still warm.

Waldorf Salad
Single serving is 1/4 of the total recipe
(includes 1 hard-cooked extra-large egg)
CALORIES 478; PROTEIN 19g; CARBS 31g; TOTAL FAT 33g; SAT FAT 3g; CHOLESTEROL 294mg; SODIUM 493mg; FIBER 5g

minute

egg and vegetable menus

meals
vegetarian

☆ baked eggs
with creamed spinach on english muffins

green salad with mushrooms and croutons

pink grapefruit with brown sugar glaze

menu gameplan

shopping list

Frozen creamed spinach

English muffins

Thick-style salsa, mild or spicy

Prewashed spring or baby greens

Presliced mushrooms (from the salad bar or produce department)

Whole-wheat croutons

Pink grapefruits

from your pantry

Large eggs

Salt and pepper

Salad dressing of choice

Brown sugar

Ground cinnamon

serves 4

beforeyoustart

Preheat the oven to 500°F to bake the eggs and glaze the grapefruit.

step 1 make the **baked eggs**

step 2 while the **eggs** are baking, assemble the **salad**

step 3 prepare the **pink grapefruit with brown sugar glaze**

step 4 **serve**

luckyforyou Creamed spinach is a major ingredient in the egg recipe, but all you have to do is thaw it.

"This whole menu, even the baked grapefruit, is pure comfort food. I'd serve this menu for breakfast, brunch, lunch, or dinner."

—minutemeals' Chef Hillary

step 1

make the **baked eggs with creamed spinach on english muffins**

2 packages (9 ounces each) frozen creamed spinach

4 large eggs

Salt and pepper to taste

4 English muffins

1/2 cup thick-style mild or spicy salsa

1. Preheat the oven to 500°F.

2. Make a slit in the end of each of the packages of frozen spinach and place them in a 2-quart Pyrex baking dish. Microwave on High for 10 minutes. Open the bags and transfer the hot spinach to the baking dish. Using the back of a soup spoon, make 4 equally spaced indentations in the spinach.

3. Break an egg into each indentation. Season the eggs with salt and pepper. Cover the baking dish with aluminum foil and bake in the conventional oven for 5 to 7 minutes, or until the eggs are set. Remove the baking dish from the oven.

4. Meanwhile, with a fork, split each of the English muffins. Toast the muffins in a toaster or toaster oven until lightly colored. Transfer 1 muffin to each of 4 dinner plates. Do not turn off the oven.

step 2

while the **eggs** are baking, assemble the **green salad with mushrooms and croutons**

1 bag (5 ounces) prewashed spring or baby greens

1 cup presliced mushrooms

1/2 cup whole-wheat croutons

1/4 cup store-bought salad dressing of choice

Place the greens, mushroom slices, and croutons in a salad bowl. Add the dressing and toss to coat. Place the bowl with 4 salad plates on the table.

step 3

prepare the **pink grapefruit with brown sugar glaze**

2 pink grapefruits

2 tablespoons packed brown sugar

1/4 teaspoon ground cinnamon

1. Cut each grapefruit in half and section the halves. Place the halves in a small baking dish.

2. Combine the brown sugar and cinnamon and sprinkle evenly over each of the grapefruit halves. Bake for 5 minutes, or until the grapefruit is warm and the sugar is slightly melted.

step 4

serve

1. Using a large spoon, scoop an egg with some of the creamed spinach under it and place it over the English muffin halves on each plate. Spoon 2 tablespoons salsa over the egg. Plate the remaining eggs and spinach and garnish with salsa in the same way.

2. When ready for dessert, serve the baked grapefruit halves, preferably still slightly warm, in 4 small bowls.

Baked Eggs with Creamed Spinach on Egg Muffins
Single serving is 1/4 of the total recipe
CALORIES 314; PROTEIN 19g; CARBS 42g; TOTAL FAT 9g; SAT FAT 3g; CHOLESTEROL 215mg; SODIUM 1144mg; FIBER 3g

★ light lemony omelet

new potatoes with garlic-herb cheese
toasted challah
melon frappes

menu
gameplan

shopping list

Frozen chopped broccoli

Lemons (for zest)

Egg whites

Thin-skinned new potatoes

Garlic-and-herb-flavored rondelé cheese

Cut-up honeydew melon

Challah bread

Very ripe honeydew melon, cut-up

Midori melon liqueur or orange juice

Fresh mint leaves (optional)

from your pantry

Large eggs or liquid egg substitute

Cream of tartar

Salt and pepper

Olive oil

Grated Parmesan cheese

Butter

Jam

Ice

Sugar

serves 4

beforeyoustart

Thaw the broccoli in the microwave oven according to the package.

step **1** cook the **light lemony omelet**

step **2** microwave the **new potatoes**

step **3** toast the **challah**

step **4** make the **melon frappes**

step **5** **serve**

lucky**for**you Egg whites come already separated and pasteurized in cartons in the dairy section of your supermarket. Pasteurized whites have been cooked slightly to remove any bacteria.

"You feel great after eating this omelet because you're not 'stuffed.'
It's the egg whites that make the difference."

—minutemeals' Chef Hillary

cook the **light lemony omelet**

1 package (10 ounces) frozen chopped broccoli, thawed

2 lemons (for grated zest)

4 large eggs or 8 ounces liquid egg substitute

4 large egg whites

1/4 teaspoon cream of tartar

Salt and pepper to taste

2 teaspoons olive oil

1/4 cup grated Parmesan cheese

1. Preheat the oven to 375°F. Thaw the broccoli in the microwave oven according to the directions on the package.

2. Grate the zest of both lemons. (You should have about 2 teaspoons.) If using whole eggs, break them into a medium bowl and beat lightly until combined.

3. In a large bowl, combine the egg whites and cream of tartar. Beat with an electric mixer on high speed until stiff peaks form when the beaters are lifted. With a large rubber spatula, gently fold in the beaten whole eggs (or egg substitute), lemon zest, and salt and pepper until well blended.

4. In a medium nonstick ovenproof skillet, heat the oil over high heat. Pour in the egg mixture, reduce the heat to medium, and cook about 3 to 5 minutes, or until the underside is slightly brown. Transfer the skillet to the oven and bake for 5 minutes.

5. Remove the skillet from the oven, spoon the broccoli over the omelet, and return the pan to the oven. Cook for 2 minutes longer, or until the eggs are set. Remove the pan from the oven and sprinkle the top with the grated Parmesan. Loosen the edges of the omelet with a rubber spatula and slide the omelet onto a large serving platter.

step 2

microwave the **new potatoes with garlic-herb cheese**

1 1/4 pounds medium thin-skinned new potatoes

Salt and pepper to taste

Garlic-and-herb-flavored rondelé cheese for serving

1. Scrub the potatoes and pierce each one several times with a skewer or a fork.

2. Place the potatoes in the microwave oven and microwave on High, turning over halfway, until tender, 4 to 6 minutes. Remove from the oven and let stand until serving time.

step 3

toast the **challah**

1 loaf challah bread

Butter, softened

Jam for serving

1. Thinly slice the challah.

2. Toast the slices in a toaster until lightly colored. Transfer the slices to a napkin-lined basket and place on the table with the butter and the jam.

step 4

make the **melon frappes**

4 cups cut-up very ripe honeydew melon

4 tablespoons Midori melon liqueur or orange juice

2 cups ice

1 tablespoon sugar

Juice of 1 lemon

In a blender, combine the melon, liqueur or orange juice, ice, sugar and lemon juice. Blend on high until smooth. Pour into stemmed glasses. If desired, serve the frappes with the meal, or chill until dessert.

step 5

serve

1. Cut the omelet into 4 equal wedges and place each on a plate.

2. Add a serving of potatoes to each plate, season with salt and pepper, and place a dollop of rondelé on top. Or serve the rondelé separately to be added by each diner at the table.

3. If the frappes have not been enjoyed already as a beverage with the meal, serve them for dessert.

Light Lemony Omelet
Single serving is 1/4 of the total recipe
CALORIES 150; PROTEIN 14g; CARBS 7g;
TOTAL FAT 8g; SAT FAT 2g; CHOLESTEROL 219mg;
SODIUM 232mg; FIBER 2g

☆ pipérade

steamed broccoli florets
mixed greens vinaigrette with feta
peach melba

menu
gameplan

shopping list

Prewashed salad greens, bagged or loose

Pre-shredded carrots (bagged, from the produce department)

Feta cheese, flavored or plain

Broccoli florets

Green peppers

Diced tomatoes with mild green chiles

Egg whites

Canned peach halves or fresh peaches or nectarines

Vanilla ice cream

Mint leaves (optional)

from your pantry

Vinaigrette dressing, store-bought or homemade

Olive oil

Onion

Garlic

Dried oregano

Eggs

Salt and pepper

Raspberry jam or preserves

serves 4

step 1 assemble the **mixed greens vinaigrette with feta**

step 2 make the **steamed broccoli florets**

step 3 cook the **pipérade**

step 4 prepare the **peach melba**

step 5 **serve**

luckyforyou The pipérade can be made ahead of time. Reheat it before adding it to the eggs.

"There's nothing retiring about pipérade. It's all about flavor, and color, and taste. The tomato-pepper topping is also wonderful on simple grilled fish."

—minutemeals' Chef Hillary

step 1

assemble the **mixed greens vinaigrette with feta**

1 bag (5 ounces) prewashed salad greens or 6 cups loose salad greens

1/2 cup pre-shredded carrots

1/4 cup crumbled feta cheese, flavored or plain

2 to 4 tablespoons vinaigrette dressing

In a large salad bowl, combine the greens, carrots, and feta. Refrigerate until serving time.

step 2

make the **steamed broccoli florets**

1 pound broccoli florets

Olive oil to taste

Place the florets in a vegetable steamer basket, place the basket in a large saucepan with 1 inch of water, and cover. Bring to a boil over high heat. Steam the florets for 5 to 7 minutes, or until crisp-tender. Transfer the florets to a serving bowl and drizzle with olive oil. Cover loosely to keep warm.

step 3

cook the **pipérade**

2 small green peppers

1 large onion

1 garlic clove

1 can (14 1/2 ounces) diced tomatoes with mild green chiles

4 teaspoons olive oil

1 teaspoon dried oregano

4 large eggs

4 large egg whites or equivalent amount liquid egg white

1 tablespoon water

Salt and pepper to taste

1. Cut the peppers into small chunks. Halve the onion and thinly slice the onion halves. Crush the garlic through a garlic press. Drain the tomatoes.

2. Make the pipérade: In a large nonstick skillet, heat 2 teaspoons of the oil over medium heat. Add the peppers, onion, garlic, and oregano and cook, stirring occasionally, for 3 minutes, or until slightly softened. Add the tomatoes and cook for 4 to 5 minutes longer, stirring occasionally, until the vegetables are tender and most of the liquid has cooked off. Transfer to a medium bowl and set aside.

3. In a medium bowl, whisk together the eggs, egg whites, water, and salt and pepper.

4. In the same skillet, heat the remaining 2 teaspoons oil over medium heat. Pour the egg mixture into the skillet and cook, lifting the edges of the eggs to allow the uncooked egg to flow underneath. Spoon the pipérade on top, cover, and cook for 2 minutes, until the vegetables are heated through and the eggs are set. Remove the pan from the heat.

step 4

prepare the **peach melba**

4 drained canned peach halves or fresh pitted peach or nectarine halves

1 pint vanilla ice cream

1/2 cup raspberry jam or preserves

1. Place 1 peach half in each of 4 glass dessert bowls. Remove the ice cream from the freezer to soften slightly.

2. In a small saucepan, heat the raspberry jam over low heat until melted.

step 5

serve

1. Cut the pipérade into wedges and place a wedge on each of 4 dinner plates. Add a serving of steamed broccoli florets and serve.

2. Add the vinaigrette to the salad and toss. Place the bowl and 4 salad plates on the table.

3. When ready for dessert, place a scoop of ice cream on each peach half. Spoon warm raspberry jam over the ice cream. Serve while the jam is still warm.

Pipérade
Single serving is 1/4 of the total recipe
CALORIES 184; PROTEIN 10g; CARBS 11g;
TOTAL FAT 9g; SAT FAT 2g; CHOLESTEROL 215mg;
SODIUM 556mg; FIBER 1g

☆ vegetable frittata

italian greens with black olives

focaccia with olive oil for dipping

orange and cream sorbet

menu **gameplan**

---

shopping list

Frozen Italian-style vegetables

Focaccia

Prewashed Italian-style mixed greens

Chopped scallions (from the salad bar)

Black olives, pitted

Orange and cream sorbet

from your pantry

Olive oil

Eggs

Dried mixed Italian herb seasoning

Salt and pepper

Grated Parmesan cheese

Vinaigrette dressing, store-bought or homemade

---

serves 4 to 6

beforeyoustart

Preheat the oven to 400°F to finish the frittata.

step 1 make the **vegetable frittata**

step 2 heat the **focaccia with olive oil for dipping**

step 3 assemble the **italian greens with black olives**

step 4 **serve**

luckyforyou It's perfectly acceptable to serve frittata hot, warm, or at room temperature.

"There's a lot to be said for serving something from the pan in which it was cooked. It's homey."

—minutemeals' Chef Joanne

step 1

make the **vegetable frittata**

2 tablespoons olive oil

1 bag (16 ounces) frozen Italian-style vegetables

1 tablespoon water

8 large eggs

1/2 teaspoon dried mixed Italian herb seasoning

1/2 teaspoon salt

Pepper to taste

3 tablespoons grated Parmesan cheese

1. Preheat the oven to 400°F.

2. In a large nonstick ovenproof skillet, heat 1 tablespoon of the olive oil over medium-high heat until hot. Add the frozen vegetables and water and cover. Cook, stirring often, until heated throughout and all the liquid has cooked off.

3. In a large bowl, beat together the eggs, herbs, salt, and pepper.

4. Add the remaining 1 tablespoon olive oil to the skillet. Pour the egg mixture over the vegetables and cook over medium-low heat, stirring every now and then, for 3 minutes,

or until the edges are set. Sprinkle the Parmesan over the top.

5. Transfer the skillet to the oven and bake for 8 to 10 minutes, or until the omelet is set.

step 2

heat the **focaccia with olive oil for dipping**

1 store-bought focaccia

Olive oil for dipping

When you transfer the frittata to the oven, slide the focaccia into the oven at the same time.

step 3

assemble the **italian greens with black olives**

1 bag (7 ounces) prewashed Italian-style mixed greens

1/4 cup chopped scallions

Pitted black olives to taste

Vinaigrette dressing of choice

Salt and pepper to taste

Place the greens in a salad bowl. Add the scallions, olives, and vinaigrette and toss. Season with salt and pepper. Place the salad bowl on the table.

step 4

serve

1. Serve the frittata from the skillet, cutting it into wedges, like a pie.

2. Place the focaccia on a bread board and place the board on the table. Serve with a small bowl of olive oil for dipping.

3. When ready for dessert, scoop the sorbet into small bowls. Serve.

Vegetable Frittata
Single serving is 1/4 of the total recipe
CALORIES 258; PROTEIN 15g; CARBS 9g;
TOTAL FAT 17g; SAT FAT 4g; CHOLESTEROL 433mg;
SODIUM 531mg; FIBER 3g

☆ welsh rarebit

green salad with olives and roasted peppers
peach cakes à la mode

menu
gameplan

shopping list

Beer

Pre-grated sharp Cheddar cheese

Fresh parsley (optional)

Jarred roasted red peppers

Prewashed spring or baby greens

Pimiento-stuffed green salad olives

Canned peaches in light syrup

Individual sponge cakes

Frozen vanilla yogurt

from your pantry

Dry mustard

Paprika

Cayenne pepper

Ground nutmeg

Butter

Eggs

Salt and pepper

Sliced whole-wheat or white bread

Vinaigrette dressing, store-bought or homemade

Amaretto liqueur or almond extract

serves 4

step	1	make the **welsh rarebit**
step	2	assemble the **salad**
step	3	prepare the **peach cakes à la mode**
step	4	**serve**

headsup
We made the rarebit in a double boiler in order to better regulate the heat as the sauce comes together. If you don't have a double boiler, here's how to improvise one. Place a metal mixing bowl over a saucepan partially filled with water. Do not fill the pan so full that the water touches the bottom of the bowl.

"Omit the eggs in the rarebit and you have a great topping for hot cooked broccoli, cauliflower, or asparagus."
—minutemeals' Chef Hillary

make the **welsh rarebit**

- 2 teaspoons dry mustard
- 2 teaspoons paprika
- 1/4 teaspoon cayenne pepper
- Pinch of ground nutmeg
- 1 cup beer
- 2 tablespoons butter
- 1 pound pre-grated sharp Cheddar cheese
- 2 large eggs
- Salt to taste
- 8 slices whole-wheat or white bread
- 1/4 cup chopped fresh parsley for garnish (optional)

1. Fill the bottom of a double boiler with water and bring barely to a simmer.

2. Meanwhile, in the top of the double boiler, put the mustard, paprika, cayenne, and nutmeg. Add the beer, a few drops at a time, stirring with a fork to make a smooth paste. Continue adding and stirring until the ingredients are well blended. Add the butter. Place the pan over the bottom filled with the barely simmering water. Cook over medium heat until the butter has melted and the mixture is quite hot.

3. Add the cheese and stir with a wooden spoon until the cheese melts.

4. Break the eggs into a small bowl and lightly beat. Add the eggs to the cheese mixture and cook, stirring, making sure not to let the mixture come to a boil. Season with salt. Cook, stirring, until the rarebit is thickened and smooth. Remove the top of the boiler from the simmering water.

5. In a toaster, lightly toast the bread.

6. Chop enough fresh parsley to measure 1/4 cup, if desired.

step 2

assemble the **green salad with olives and roasted peppers**

- 1 jar (4 ounces) roasted red peppers
- 1 bag (5 ounces) prewashed spring or baby greens
- 1/2 cup pimiento-stuffed green salad olives
- 2 to 4 tablespoons vinaigrette dressing
- Salt and pepper to taste

1. Drain the roasted peppers and cut into thin strips.

2. In a salad bowl, combine the greens, olives, pepper strips, vinaigrette, and salt and pepper. Toss to coat. Place the bowl with 4 salad plates on the table.

step 3

prepare the **peach cakes à la mode**

- 1 can (16 ounces) peaches in light syrup, undrained
- 2 tablespoons amaretto liqueur or 1/4 teaspoon almond extract
- 4 store-bought individual sponge cakes
- Frozen vanilla yogurt

In a medium bowl, combine the peaches in their syrup with the amaretto or almond extract. Refrigerate until ready to serve.

step 4

serve

1. Cut each piece of toast in half crosswise and place 4 halves on each of 4 dinner plates. Spoon the hot cheese sauce over the top and sprinkle with parsley, if desired. Serve.

2. When ready for dessert, place a sponge cake on each of 4 dessert plates. Spoon the peaches with their juices over the top, add a small scoop of frozen yogurt, and serve.

Welsh Rarebit
Single serving is 1/4 of the total recipe
CALORIES 698; PROTEIN 38g; CARBS 29g;
TOTAL FAT 49g; SAT FAT 29g; CHOLESTEROL 241mg;
SODIUM 1178mg; FIBER 4g

☆ cajun corn, rice, and red beans

okra with spicy tomatoes
frosted angel food cake with toasted coconut

menu
gameplan

shopping list

Green pepper

Red pepper

Red beans, such as kidney beans

Frozen corn kernels

Diced tomatoes with mild green chiles

Frozen okra

Shredded coconut

Angel food cake

Vanilla frosting

from your pantry

Onion

Garlic

Olive oil

Cajun seasoning or chili powder

Instant white rice

Vegetable broth

Salt and pepper

Hot pepper sauce (optional)

serves 4

step 1 make the **cajun corn, rice, and red beans**

step 2 cook the **okra with spicy tomatoes**

step 3 prepare the **angel food cake**

step 4 **serve**

 This entrée also makes an excellent side dish.

"What's intriguing to me about this recipe is just how basic the ingredients are. Corn, rice, and beans have sustained people for centuries."

—minutemeals' Chef Joanne

step 1

make the **cajun corn, rice, and red beans**

- 1 large green pepper
- 1 large red pepper
- 1 medium onion
- 2 garlic cloves
- 1 can (15½ ounces) red beans, such as kidney beans
- 1 tablespoon olive oil
- 1 teaspoon Cajun seasoning or chili powder
- 2 cups instant white rice
- 1 can (14½ ounces) vegetable broth
- 1 package (16 ounces) frozen corn kernels
- Salt and pepper to taste
- 2 to 6 drops hot pepper sauce, or to taste (optional)

1. Chop both peppers to measure 1 cup each. Chop the onion to measure 1 cup. Slice the garlic. Rinse and drain the beans.

2. In a large deep heavy skillet, heat the olive oil over high heat until hot. Add the peppers, onion, garlic, and Cajun seasoning. Stir to coat with the oil and cook for 3 minutes, until softened slightly.

3. Add the rice and stir to coat. Add the broth and bring to a boil, covered. Stir in the corn and beans and cover the pan. Remove the pan from the heat and let stand for 5 minutes. Season with salt and pepper and hot pepper sauce, if desired.

step 2

cook the **okra with spicy tomatoes**

- 1 can (14½ ounces) diced tomatoes with mild green chiles
- 1 package (10 ounces) frozen sliced okra

In a large saucepan, combine the tomatoes and okra. Bring to a boil, covered, over medium-high heat, reduce the heat to a simmer, and cook, separating the slices of frozen okra with a spoon, for about 8 to 10 minutes, or until the okra is cooked and the mixture is heated through. Transfer to a serving bowl, cover to keep warm, and place on the table.

step 3

prepare the **frosted angel food cake with toasted coconut**

- 1 cup shredded coconut
- 1 store-bought angel food cake
- 1 container (16 ounces) vanilla frosting

1. Spread the coconut on a Pyrex pie plate or paper plate and microwave on High for 2 minutes. Stir and microwave for 3 to 4 minutes stirring every minute to make sure it is evenly golden. Remove and let cool.

2. Place the cake on a cake platter or large plate. Frost the sides and the top. Sprinkle the toasted coconut all over the cake, pressing it lightly on with your hands.

step 4

serve

1. Place the skillet on the table and spoon portions directly onto 4 dinner plates. Serve the okra alongside.

2. When ready for dessert, cut the angel food cake into slices, place on 4 dessert plates, and serve.

Cajun Corn, Rice, and Red Beans
Single serving is ¼ of the total recipe
CALORIES 350; PROTEIN 13g; CARBS 70g;
TOTAL FAT 6g; SAT FAT 1g; CHOLESTEROL 0mg;
SODIUM 420mg; FIBER 11g

curried rice and vegetables
pappadams
flan with raisins

menu
gameplan

shopping list

Jasmine rice

Frozen mixed vegetables, such as peas and carrots

Peanuts

Cilantro

Mango chutney (optional)

Pappadams

Dark raisins

Dark rum or orange juice

Individual flans

from your pantry

Onion

Garlic

Olive oil

Curry powder

Salt and pepper

Peanut or vegetable oil

serves 4

step **1** make the **curried rice and vegetables**

step **2** fry the **pappadams**

step **3** prepare the **flan with raisins**

step **4** **serve**

headsup

A deep-fry thermometer takes the guesswork out of deep-frying. If you don't have one, there's another way to test the hotness of the oil. Carefully drop a bread cube into the oil. If the cube fries in 30 seconds, you can assume the oil is about 375°F, hot enough to deep-fry.

"Want to 'stretch' this rice-and-vegetable entrée? Add 1 cup rinsed and drained chickpeas or diced tempeh."

—minutemeals' Chef Hillary

step 1

make the **curried rice and vegetables**

1 medium onion

2 garlic cloves

1 tablespoon olive oil

1¼ cups jasmine rice

1 to 3 teaspoons curry powder

Salt and pepper to taste

2¾ cups water

1 (10-ounce) package frozen mixed vegetables, such as peas and carrots

½ cup salted peanuts

1 tablespoon fresh cilantro leaves

Mango chutney for serving (optional)

1. Coarsely chop the onion to measure 1 cup. Slice the garlic.

2. In a heavy deep nonstick skillet, heat the oil over high heat. Add the onion and garlic and cook, stirring often, about 2 minutes, or until slightly softened.

3. Stir in the rice, curry powder, and salt and pepper. Stir in the water and bring to a boil, covered. Reduce the heat to low, and cook for 10 minutes, or until the rice is tender and the water is absorbed.

4. Stir in the mixed vegetables. Cover and let stand to heat through.

5. Transfer the rice mixture to a serving bowl and sprinkle with the peanuts and cilantro. Keep warm, partially covered.

step 2

fry the **pappadams**

½ cup peanut or vegetable oil

1 package (4 ounces) pappadams

1. In a heavy deep cast-iron skillet, heat the oil over high heat until hot. (See "heads up" for tips on determining the temperature of oil.)

2. Fry the pappadams according to the directions on the package; drain on paper towels. Transfer the drained pappadams to a large plate and place the plate on the table.

step 3

prepare the **flan with raisins**

½ cup dark raisins

2 tablespoons dark rum or orange juice

4 individual flans

1. Place the raisins in a small bowl and pour in the rum or orange juice. Let stand until serving time.

2. Place a flan in each of 4 dessert bowls.

step 4

serve

1. Spoon curried rice into 4 pasta or soup bowls and serve with the mango chutney as an accompaniment, if desired. Serve with the pappadams.

2. When ready for dessert, spoon some of the raisins and soaking liquid over each flan. Serve.

Curried Rice and Vegetables
Single serving is ¼ of the total recipe
CALORIES 436; PROTEIN 13g; CARBS 63g; TOTAL FAT 14g; SAT FAT 0g; CHOLESTEROL 0mg; SODIUM 187mg; FIBER 3g

hoppin' john
(black-eyed peas and rice)

buttered succotash

buttermilk biscuits

mint chocolate chip ice cream with chocolate mints

menu gameplan

serves 4

step 1 make the **hoppin' john**

step 2 heat the **buttermilk biscuits**

step 3 cook the **buttered succotash**

step 4 **serve**

shopping list

Black-eyed peas

Buttermilk biscuits

Frozen succotash

Mint chocolate chip ice cream

Chocolate mint thins

from the salad bar

Shredded carrots (or from the produce department)

Chopped scallions

from your pantry

Onion

Garlic

Olive oil

Instant white rice

Vegetable broth

Salt and pepper

Butter

headsup You'll realize a sizable savings on sodium, almost 950 milligrams, by using frozen black-eyed peas to make Hoppin' John. Look for them in 1-pound packages in the freezer section of larger supermarkets.

"I love recipes with lore. Hoppin' John is meant to bring you good luck if you eat it before noon on New Year's Day." —minutemeals' Chef Hillary

make the **hoppin' john**

- 1 small onion
- 2 garlic cloves
- 2 cans (15 1/2 ounces each) black-eyed peas
- 1 tablespoon olive oil
- 2 cups instant white rice
- 1 can (14 1/2 ounces) vegetable broth
- 1 cup shredded carrots
- 1/2 cup chopped scallions
- Salt and pepper to taste

1. Chop the onion. Peel the garlic cloves. Rinse and drain the black-eyed peas.

2. In a large deep skillet, heat the olive oil over high heat until hot. Add the onion and crush the garlic cloves directly into the pan. Cook, stirring often, for 3 to 5 minutes, or until the onion is soft and slightly browned.

3. Add the rice and stir to coat. Add the broth and bring to a boil, covered. Add the black-eyed peas and carrots and stir until incorporated. Cover, remove the pan from the heat, and let stand about 5 minutes, until the liquid is absorbed. Fluff with a fork, stir in the scallions, and season with salt and pepper.

step 2

heat the **buttermilk biscuits**

- 1 package store-bought buttermilk biscuits

Place the biscuits in a toaster oven to heat until serving time.

step 3

cook the **buttered succotash**

- 1 package (10 ounces) frozen succotash
- 1 tablespoon softened butter

Cook the succotash in a medium saucepan according to the directions on the package. Drain, transfer to a serving dish, and top with the butter. Toss until melted. Place the dish on the table.

step 4

serve

1. Spoon the Hoppin' John onto 4 dinner plates and serve, accompanied by the succotash and biscuits.

2. When ready for dessert, scoop the ice cream into dessert bowls and garnish each with chocolate mint thins. Serve, with additional chocolate thins, if desired.

Hoppin' John
Single serving is 1/4 of the total recipe
CALORIES 281; PROTEIN 15g; CARBS 54g; TOTAL FAT 4g; SAT FAT 1g; CHOLESTEROL 0mg; SODIUM 1434mg; FIBER; 9g

vegetable and noodle stir-fry
with tofu
fruit kabobs with yogurt

menu
gameplan

shopping list

Canned pineapple chunks in juice

Strawberries

Bamboo skewers

Vanilla yogurt

Snow peas
(from the salad bar)

Yellow summer squash

Red pepper

Ginger

Firm tofu

Thin egg noodles or
angel hair pasta

from your pantry

Ground cinnamon

Salt

Garlic

Vegetable broth

Lite soy sauce

Cornstarch

Peanut or vegetable oil

serves 4

beforeyoustart

Bring a large pan of water, covered, to a boil over high heat to cook the noodles.

step	1	assemble the **fruit kabobs with yogurt**

step	2	make the **noodles;** cook the **stir-fry**

step	3	**serve**

luckyforyou Thin pasta, especially fresh, but also dried, is *very* quick cooking. The risk, in fact, is in overcooking it!

"It wasn't so long ago that Chinese-style recipes called for a lot of oil for stir-frying. It's not that way anymore." —minutemeals' Chef Hillary

step 1

assemble the **fruit kabobs with yogurt**

1 can (20 ounces) pineapple chunks in juice

1 pint strawberries

8 bamboo skewers (each 10 inches long)

1 container (8 ounces) vanilla yogurt

Ground cinnamon

1. Drain the pineapple. Hull and rinse the strawberries.

2. Thread each skewer with fruit, alternating the pineapple chunks and strawberries. Place on a plate.

3. Fill a small glass bowl with the vanilla yogurt and sprinkle with cinnamon. Refrigerate until serving time.

step 2

make the **noodles;** cook the **vegetable and noodle stir-fry with tofu**

3 quarts water

Salt to taste

1/2 pound stringed snow peas

1 medium-large yellow summer squash

1 large red pepper

2 garlic cloves

1-inch piece fresh ginger

8 ounces firm tofu

1 cup vegetable broth or water

1/4 cup lite soy sauce

1 1/2 tablespoons cornstarch

1 tablespoon peanut or vegetable oil

8 ounces very thin egg noodles or angel hair pasta

1. Pour the water into a large saucepan, salt light, and cover. Bring to a boil over high heat.

2. Meanwhile, make the stir-fry: Stem and string the snow peas, if necessary. Trim and slice the squash 1/4 inch thick. Cut the pepper into 1-inch pieces. Thinly slice the garlic. Grate the ginger. Cut the tofu into 1/2-inch pieces.

3. In a cup, stir together the broth or water, soy sauce, and cornstarch.

4. Heat the oil in a large nonstick wok or deep skillet over high heat. Add the snow peas, squash, red pepper, garlic, and ginger and stir-fry for 3 to 4 minutes, or until the vegetables are crisp-tender. Add the tofu and stir-fry for 1 to 2 minutes, or until heated through.

5. Stir the cornstarch mixture to recombine it and add it to the wok. Cook, stirring constantly, for 2 minutes, or until the sauce is thickened and bubbly. Remove the pan from the heat and keep warm.

6. Add the noodles to the boiling water and stir to separate. Cook for 3 minutes, or until tender but still *al dente*. Remove 1 cup of the cooking liquid and reserve. Drain the noodles and return to the pan.

7. Add the vegetable stir-fry to the noodles and some of the reserved cooking water, if desired, and toss well.

step 3

serve

1. Divide the stir-fry evenly among 4 deep bowls and serve with chopsticks, if desired.

2. When ready for dessert, place the plate of kabobs on the table, with dessert plates and the yogurt sauce to be used either as a dipping sauce or topping.

Vegetable and Noodle Stir-Fry with Tofu
Single serving is 1/4 of the total recipe
CALORIES 362; PROTEIN 16g; CARBS 61g;
TOTAL FAT 7g; SAT FAT 1g; CHOLESTEROL 0mg;
SODIUM 583mg; FIBER 4g

⭐ creamed mushrooms and vegetables
on biscuits

lemony chickpea and artichoke salad

fruit platter with shortbread cookies

menu
gameplan

shopping list

Refrigerated buttermilk biscuits, Hungry Jack brand

Portobello mushrooms, sliced (from the produce department)

Fresh rosemary

Frozen mixed baby sweet peas and pearl onions

Light cream

Dry sherry

Chickpeas

Jarred marinated artichoke hearts, quartered or chopped

Lemon (for juice)

Plums

Red apples

Red grapes

Shortbread cookies

from your pantry

Butter

Dried thyme

Vegetable broth

All-purpose flour

Ground nutmeg

Freshly ground black pepper

Salt

serves 4

beforeyoustart
Preheat the oven to 400°F.

step	1	heat the **biscuits**
step	2	make the **creamed mushrooms and vegetables**
step	3	assemble the **lemony chickpea and artichoke salad**
step	4	assemble the **fruit platter**
step	5	**serve**

luckyforyou Portobellos come ready-to-use—cleaned and sliced—in most supermarket produce departments.

"You could also serve the creamed mushrooms and vegetables over pasta, with a dusting of Parmesan on top. Fresh spinach pasta would be good."

—minutemeals' Chef Miriam

step 1

heat the **biscuits**

> 8 biscuits from a 6-ounce package of Hungry Jack Buttermilk Biscuits (reserve the remaining 2 biscuits for another time)

Arrange the biscuits on a baking sheet according to the directions on the package. When the oven is just about at 400°F, place the baking sheet on the upper rack. Bake for 11 to 14 minutes, until the biscuits are golden brown.

step 2

make the **creamed mushrooms and vegetables**

> 2 tablespoons butter
>
> 2 packages (6 ounces each) sliced portobello mushrooms
>
> 1 teaspoon chopped fresh rosemary
>
> 1/2 teaspoon dried thyme
>
> 1 package (16 ounces) frozen mixed baby sweet peas and pearl onions
>
> 3/4 cup vegetable broth
>
> 3/4 cup light cream
>
> 3 tablespoons all-purpose flour
>
> 2 tablespoons dry sherry
>
> Ground nutmeg to taste
>
> Freshly ground pepper and salt to taste

1. In a large deep nonstick skillet, melt the butter over medium-high heat. Add the mushrooms and toss. Increase the heat to high and cook, tossing frequently, for 2 minutes.

Reduce the heat to medium and cook until the mushrooms start to release their liquid, 3 to 4 minutes. While the mushrooms cook, chop the rosemary.

2. Stir in the rosemary and thyme. Stir in the frozen vegetables, increase the heat, and cook, stirring occasionally, for 5 to 6 minutes, until some of the moisture from the vegetables has evaporated.

3. While the vegetables are cooking, shake the vegetable broth, light cream, and flour in a clean jar with a tight-fitting lid. Stir it into the vegetable mixture, bring it to a simmer, and cook, stirring occasionally, until thickened, about 3 minutes.

4. Stir in the sherry, a generous pinch of nutmeg, and a very generous amount of fresh pepper. Taste and add salt, if necessary.

step 3

assemble the **lemony chickpea and artichoke salad**

> 1 can (15 1/2 ounces) chickpeas
>
> 1 jar (6 1/2 ounces) marinated quartered or chopped artichoke hearts
>
> Juice of 1/2 lemon
>
> Freshly ground pepper to taste

1. Rinse and drain the chickpeas.

2. In a salad bowl, place the chickpeas and the artichokes and their liquid. Stick a fork into the lemon

half and squeeze the juice over the chickpeas and artichokes. Season with fresh pepper and toss to mix well.

step 4

assemble the **fruit platter**

> 4 ripe plums
>
> 2 crisp red apples
>
> 2 bunches red grapes

Rinse the fruits, shake dry, and arrange on a platter. Chill until serving time.

step 5

serve

1. Split the hot biscuits and arrange 4 halves on each of 4 dinner plates. Spoon some of the creamed mushrooms and vegetables over the biscuits.

2. Serve the biscuits with the salad.

3. When ready for dessert, place the fruit platter, cookies, and dessert plates on the table.

Creamed Mushrooms and Vegetables on Biscuits
Single serving is 1/4 of the total recipe
(includes 2 whole biscuits per serving)
CALORIES 421; PROTEIN 10g; CARBS 46g;
TOTAL FAT 23g; SAT FAT 7g; CHOLESTEROL 45mg;
SODIUM 884mg; FIBER 2g

eggplant parmigiana

insalata mista

rosemary focaccia

spumoni ice cream

menu
gameplan

serves 4

beforeyoustart

Preheat the broiler to grill the eggplant and heat focaccia.

| step | 1 | assemble the **insalata mista** |

| step | 2 | cook the **eggplant parmigiana** |

| step | 3 | heat the **rosemary focaccia** |

| step | 4 | **serve** |

shopping list

Prewashed Italian-style salad greens

Cucumber slices (from the salad bar)

Jarred marinated mushrooms

Eggplants

Fresh basil

Pre-shredded part-skim mozzarella

Grated Parmigiano-Reggiano cheese

Focaccia (Italian flatbread, from specialty breads section of most supermarkets)

Spumoni ice cream

from your pantry

Olive oil

Balsamic vinegar

Salt and pepper

Marinara sauce, store-bought

Dried rosemary

luckyforyou Some supermarket bakeries sell focaccia already herbed or seasoned—ready for heating, in other words.

"I used to think twice about making Eggplant Parmigiana—too much time and too many calories. Turning it into a minutemeal made it doable again."

—minutemeals' Chef Miriam

step 1

assemble the **insalata mista**

1 bag (about 7 ounces) prewashed Italian-style salad greens

1/2 cup thin cucumber slices

1 jar (8 ounces) marinated mushrooms

2 tablespoons olive oil

1 tablespoon balsamic vinegar

Salt and pepper to taste

Arrange the greens in a large shallow salad bowl. Top with the cucumbers and mushrooms, including a little of the marinating liquid, if desired. Add the olive oil and vinegar and salt and pepper and toss to combine. Place the salad bowl on the table.

step 2

cook the **eggplant parmigiana**

Olive oil for brushing

2 medium eggplants

Salt and pepper to taste

2 cups store-bought marinara sauce

1/3 cup chopped fresh basil

8 ounces (2 cups) pre-shredded part-skim mozzarella

1/3 cup grated Parmigiano-Reggiano cheese, plus additional for serving

1. Preheat the broiler. Brush a jelly-roll pan or large shallow baking pan with olive oil.

2. Rinse and trim the eggplants. With a sharp knife, cut them into 1/3-inch-thick slices. Brush the slices on both sides with oil, season with salt and pepper, and arrange in one layer on the prepared pan. Broil for 4 or 5 minutes, or until golden brown. (Monitor the broiling and rearrange the slices so that they cook evenly.) Turn the slices over and broil for 4 or 5 minutes.

3. Meanwhile, in a medium saucepan, heat the marinara sauce.

4. Chop enough basil to measure 1/3 cup; stir the basil into the sauce.

5. Spoon the hot marinara sauce over the eggplant slices, and sprinkle evenly with the mozzarella and grated Parmesan. Place the pan back under broiler just until the cheese melts, about 3 minutes.

step 3

heat the **rosemary focaccia**

1 focaccia

Olive oil for brushing

Dried rosemary

1. Preheat the oven to 350°F.

2. Brush the focaccia lightly with olive oil and sprinkle with dried rosemary. Place on a cookie sheet and heat until warmed through.

step 4

serve

1. Divide the eggplant slices among 4 dinner plates. Serve with additional grated Parmesan at the table.

2. Place the focaccia on the table, with additional olive oil, for dipping, if desired.

3. When ready for dessert, scoop the ice cream into 4 small bowls and serve.

Eggplant Parmigiana
Single serving is 1/4 of the total recipe
CALORIES 421; PROTEIN 21g; CARBS 36g;
TOTAL FAT 23g; SAT FAT 8g; CHOLESTEROL 41mg;
SODIUM 851mg; FIBER 8g

gratinéed stuffed portobello mushrooms

tricolor salad

breadsticks

marble pound cake with amaretto chocolate sauce

menu gameplan

serves 4

step 1 cook the **gratinéed stuffed portobello mushrooms**

step 2 assemble the **tricolor salad**

step 3 prepare the **marble pound cake**

step 4 serve

shopping list

Zucchini

Red pepper

Prepared pesto sauce

Portobello mushroom caps, stemmed (from the produce department)

Pre-shredded part-skim mozzarella

Chickpeas

Grape tomatoes

Prewashed Italian-style salad greens

Marble pound cake

Instant whipped cream (optional)

Breadsticks

Red or sweet white onion slices (from the salad bar)

from your pantry

Garlic

Olive oil

Salt and pepper

Italian-style seasoned breadcrumbs

Vinaigrette dressing, store-bought or homemade

Amaretto liqueur or almond extract

Chocolate sauce

luckyforyou Sun-dried tomato pesto makes a great substitute for the basil pesto in the stuffing.

"You can use the large white 'stuffing mushrooms' (large domestic button mushrooms) in place of the portobellos. Watch the cooking time though."

—minutemeals' Chef Hillary

step 1

cook the **gratinéed stuffed portobello mushrooms**

- 2 garlic cloves
- 3 tablespoons olive oil
- Salt and pepper to taste
- 1 medium zucchini
- 1 medium red pepper
- 1/3 cup store-bought pesto sauce
- 1/2 cup Italian-style seasoned breadcrumbs
- 4 extra-large stemmed portobello mushroom caps
- 1 package (8 ounces) pre-shredded part-skim mozzarella

1. Preheat the broiler. Place a sheet of aluminum foil on the broiler pan rack.

2. Finely chop the garlic. In a small bowl, stir together the olive oil and garlic and season with salt and pepper.

3. Chop the zucchini and red pepper and place in a medium bowl. Add 2 teaspoons of the garlic oil. Spread the oiled vegetables on the prepared pan and broil for 3 minutes. Lift the foil from the rack and return the vegetables to the medium bowl. Add the pesto and crumbs and stir to combine well.

4. Place the mushroom caps, open side down, on the broiler pan rack and brush with garlic oil. Broil for 2 to 3 minutes. Turn, brush the mushrooms with the remaining garlic oil, and broil for 3 minutes.

5. Divide the stuffing evenly among the mushrooms, spooning it in and gently patting it down. Sprinkle with the mozzarella. Broil until the cheese has just melted and starts to brown. Turn off broiler and keep mushrooms warm while making the salad.

step 2

assemble the **tricolor salad**

- 1 can (15 ounces) chickpeas
- 1 cup grape tomatoes
- 1 bag (11 ounces) prewashed Italian-style salad greens
- 1/4 cup red or sweet white onion slices
- 3 tablespoons vinaigrette dressing

1. Rinse and drain the chickpeas. Rinse the grape tomatoes and pat dry.

2. Place the salad greens in a large salad bowl, add the chickpeas, tomatoes, onion slices, and vinaigrette and toss. Place the bowl on the table.

step 3

prepare the **marble pound cake with amaretto chocolate sauce**

- 1 jar (4 ounces) quality chocolate sauce
- 2 tablespoons amaretto liqueur or 1/4 teaspoon almond extract
- 4 slices store-bought marble pound cake
- Instant whipped cream (optional)

In a small microwave-safe bowl, combine the chocolate sauce and liqueur. Microwave on High for 1 minute, or until warm.

step 4

serve

1. Place 1 stuffed portobello on each of 4 dinner plates. Serve with the salad and breadsticks.

2. When ready for dessert, place a slice of pound cake on each plate. Spoon hot chocolate sauce over the top, and serve with whipped cream, if desired.

Gratinéed Stuffed Portobello Mushrooms
Single serving is 1/4 of the total recipe
CALORIES 459; PROTEIN 23g; CARBS 24g;
TOTAL FAT 32g; SAT FAT 8g; CHOLESTEROL 34mg;
SODIUM 695mg; FIBER 3g

cheddary micro-baked potatoes

spinach salad with egg

frozen chocolate yogurt
and orange cookies

shopping list

Baking potatoes

Pre-shredded extra-sharp
Cheddar, Monterey Jack,
or Swiss cheese

Reduced-fat sour cream

Oil-packed sun-dried
tomatoes

Cherry or grape tomatoes

Prewashed baby spinach
leaves

Red wine vinegar vinaigrette
dressing

Frozen chocolate yogurt

Orange cookies

from the salad bar

Chopped scallions

Peeled hard-cooked eggs

from your pantry

Salt and freshly ground
black pepper

Croutons

serves 4

| step | 1 | make the **cheddary micro-baked potatoes** |

| step | 2 | assemble the **spinach salad with egg** |

| step | 3 | **serve** |

 There's time in this menu to
grate a piece of Cheddar if
that's all you have in the fridge.

"Even after the most exhausting day, you can still get it together enough to make this! And you'll be glad you did." —minutemeals' Chef Hillary

make the **cheddary micro-baked potatoes**

4 medium (8 ounces each) baking potatoes

1¹/₂ cups pre-shredded extra-sharp Cheddar, Monterey Jack, or Swiss cheese

¹/₂ cup reduced-fat sour cream

¹/₄ cup chopped scallions

¹/₄ teaspoon salt

¹/₈ teaspoon freshly ground black pepper

1. Pierce the potatoes in several places with a fork. Place 1 potato in the center of the microwave tray and the other 3 around it like spokes on a wheel. Microwave on High for 14 to 16 minutes, or until tender. Carefully slit each potato and allow to cool 1 minute.

2. While the potatoes bake, in a medium bowl, stir together well the Cheddar, sour cream, scallions, salt, and pepper.

assemble the **spinach salad with egg**

2 tablespoons chopped oil-packed sun-dried tomatoes

¹/₂ cup cherry or grape tomatoes

1 bag (5 ounces) prewashed baby spinach leaves

2 tablespoons croutons

3 tablespoons store-bought red wine vinegar vinaigrette dressing

2 peeled hard-cooked eggs

1. Chop enough sun-dried tomatoes, drained, to measure 2 tablespoons.

2. Rinse the grape tomatoes and pat dry.

3. Place the spinach, grape tomatoes, sun-dried tomatoes, and croutons in a large salad bowl. Add the vinaigrette and toss.

4. Quarter the eggs and place the wedges on the salad. Place the bowl on the table.

serve

1. Place each potato on a dinner plate. With the back of a fork, mash the insides of each. Top the halves with the Cheddar mixture, dividing it evenly among the potatoes, and stir it in to combine. Serve the potatoes with the salad.

2. When ready for dessert, scoop the frozen yogurt into dessert bowls and serve it with the cookies.

Cheddary Micro-Baked Potatoes
Single serving is ¹/₄ of the total recipe
CALORIES 358; PROTEIN 16g; CARBS 38g;
TOTAL FAT 16g; SAT FAT 10g; CHOLESTEROL 49mg;
SODIUM 454mg; FIBER 3g

microwave zucchini lasagne
garlic bread
pound cake with lemon curd and raspberries

shopping list

Zucchini

Part-skim ricotta

Dried seasoned bread stuffing, such as Pepperidge Farm

Grated mozzarella

Ready-to-heat garlic bread

Quick-thaw frozen raspberries

Pound cake

Lemon curd

from your pantry

Egg

Dried basil

Salt and pepper

Marinara sauce, store-bought

serves 4

beforeyoustart
Preheat the oven to 350°F to heat the garlic bread.

step	1	make the **microwave zucchini lasagne**
step	2	heat the **garlic bread**
step	3	prepare the **pound cake**
step	4	**serve**

luckyforyou There's a really simple way to up the flavor in this lasagne: Use marinara sauce with roasted garlic or pesto.

"I'll never forget the 5-hour lasagnes I used to make! This noodle-less variation is fun to make and tasty, not a chore at all."
—minutemeals' Chef Hillary

step 1

make the **microwave zucchini lasagne**

4 medium zucchini

1 large egg

1 container (8 ounces) part-skim ricotta

2 teaspoons dried basil

Salt and pepper to taste

1 jar (26 ounces) store-bought marinara sauce

2 cups dried seasoned bread stuffing, such as Pepperidge Farm

8 ounces grated mozzarella cheese

1. Slice the zucchini into very thin rounds using the slicing blade on the side of a standard box grater.

2. In a medium bowl, blend together the egg, ricotta, basil, and salt and pepper.

3. Spread 1 cup of the marinara sauce over the bottom of a 13-×9-×2-inch baking dish. Arrange half the zucchini slices over the sauce. Spread half the ricotta mixture over the zucchini. Sprinkle with 1 cup stuffing, followed by half the mozzarella and 1 cup marinara sauce.

4. Repeat with a layer of the remaining zucchini, ricotta mixture, stuffing, and sauce. Sprinkle with the remaining mozzarella.

5. Cover the dish with vented plastic wrap and microwave on High for 10 to 12 minutes. Let rest for 2 minutes before cutting and serving.

step 2

heat the **garlic bread**

1 ready-to-heat garlic bread

1. Preheat the oven to 350°F.

2. Heat the garlic bread according to the directions on the package.

step 3

prepare the **pound cake with lemon curd and raspberries**

1 bag (12 ounces) quick-thaw frozen raspberries

4 slices store-bought pound cake

1 jar (12 ounces) lemon curd

Thaw the raspberries in the microwave oven according to the directions on the package.

step 4

serve

1. Place the lasagne on the table. Serve it directly from the baking dish, cutting it into squares.

2. Place the garlic bread on a bread board and serve while hot.

3. When ready for dessert, place a slice of pound cake on each of 4 dessert plates. Spoon lemon curd on top or alongside and garnish the plates with raspberries. Serve any remaining raspberries separately, if desired.

Microwave Zucchini Lasagne
Single serving is ¼ of the total recipe
CALORIES 568; PROTEIN 29g; CARBS 43g; TOTAL FAT 32g; SAT FAT 13g; CHOLESTEROL 111mg; SODIUM 1623mg; FIBER 5g

vegetable and cashew stir-fry

quick white rice

lichee nuts and almond cookies

menu gameplan

shopping list

Frozen edamame
(green soybeans, available
in freezer sections in most
supermarkets)

Gingerroot

Roasted unsalted cashews

Canned lichee nuts

Almond cookies

from the salad bar

Red pepper slices

Broccoli florets (or from the
produce department)

Shredded carrots (or from the
produce department)

Chopped scallions

from your pantry

Instant rice

Vegetable broth

Lite soy sauce

Cornstarch

Peanut or vegetable oil

serves 4

step **1** prepare **quick white rice**

step **2** make the **vegetable and cashew stir-fry**

step **3** **serve**

 Supermarkets have more
and more ready-to-cook
ingredients in the produce department. Buy as many of
them as you can for a recipe like this.

"I know cashew nuts are expensive. You can use almonds instead. Toast them ahead of time for maximum flavor."

—minutemeals' Chef Hillary

step 1

prepare **quick white rice**

2 cups instant rice

In a medium saucepan, prepare the rice according to the directions on the package. Let stand until ready to serve.

step 2

make the **vegetable and cashew stir-fry**

2 cups red pepper slices

2 cups frozen edamame (green soybeans)

1 knob (1 inch) gingerroot

3/4 cup vegetable broth or water

1/4 cup lite soy sauce

1 tablespoon cornstarch

1 tablespoon peanut or vegetable oil

2 cups broccoli florets

1 cup shredded carrots

1/2 cup roasted unsalted cashews

1 cup chopped scallions

1. Coarsely chop the red pepper slices. Rinse the edamame under cold water and drain. Chop the ginger.

2. In a cup, stir together the broth, soy sauce, and cornstarch.

3. Heat the oil in a large nonstick wok or deep skillet over high heat. Add the red pepper, edamame, broccoli, carrots, and ginger and stir-fry for 3 to 4 minutes, or until the florets are crisp-tender.

4. Add the cashews and scallions and stir-fry for 2 minutes.

5. Stir the broth mixture to recombine and add it to the vegetables. Bring to a boil, covered, and stirring, and cook, stirring, for 2 minutes, or until the sauce is thickened and bubbly and the mixture is heated through.

step 3

serve

1. Divide the rice evenly among 4 bowls and top with the vegetable stir-fry.

2. When ready for dessert, drain the lichee nuts. Serve them in 4 small bowls with the almond cookies as an accompaniment.

Vegetable and Cashew Stir-Fry
Single serving is 1/4 of the total recipe
(includes a serving of rice)

CALORIES 487; PROTEIN 27g; CARBS 58; TOTAL FAT 19g; SAT FAT 3g; CHOLESTEROL 0mg; SODIUM 556mg; FIBER 10g

vegetarian
sloppy joes
on whole-wheat buns
potato salad and cole slaw
s'mores

serves 4

shopping list

Green pepper

Textured vegetable protein

Tomato paste

Whole-wheat hamburger buns

Cole slaw
(from the deli counter)

Potato salad
(from the deli counter)

Marshmallow fluff

Graham crackers

Semisweet chocolate bar

from your pantry

Onion

Olive oil

Garlic

Ketchup

Red wine vinegar

Salt and pepper

step 1 make the **vegetarian sloppy joes**

step 2 plate the **potato salad and cole slaw**

step 3 make the **s'mores**

step 4 **serve**

luckyforyou This Sloppy Joe mixture easily turns into chili. Just add drained and rinsed red beans, chili powder, and chopped cilantro.

"Sometimes you have to try an ingredient like textured vegetable protein to find out how viable it is. My whole family likes these Sloppy Joes."

—minutemeals' Chef Hillary

make the **vegetarian sloppy joes on whole-wheat buns**

- 1 small onion
- 1 green pepper
- 2 teaspoons olive oil
- 2 garlic cloves
- 2 packages (12 ounces each) textured vegetable protein
- 1 can (6 ounces) tomato paste
- 1/4 cup ketchup
- 1 cup water
- 1 tablespoon red wine vinegar
- Salt and pepper to taste
- 4 whole-wheat hamburger buns

1. Chop the onion and green pepper.

2. Heat the oil in a large deep non-stick skillet over medium-high heat. Crush the garlic through a garlic press into the pan, add chopped onion and green pepper, and cook, stirring often, for 3 to 5 minutes, or until the onion is soft. Crumble the vegetable protein as you would chopped meat into the skillet. Cook, stirring, 2 minutes or until heated through and the mixture is well combined.

3. Add the tomato paste, ketchup, water, and vinegar and season with salt and pepper. Bring to a boil, covered, and simmer for 5 minutes, or until thickened.

4. While the mixture cooks, split the buns and toast them in a toaster oven until warm.

plate the **potato salad and cole slaw**

- 1 pound store-bought cole slaw
- 1 pound store-bought potato salad

Plate each of the salads in a separate bowl and place on the table.

make the **s'mores**

- Marshmallow fluff
- 8 graham crackers
- 4 ounces semisweet chocolate

Spread marshmallow fluff on each of 4 graham crackers. Place 1 ounce chocolate on top and cover with a remaining graham cracker. Place the cookies on a microwave-safe plate and microwave on High for 1 minute, until the chocolate is melted.

serve

1. Place a hamburger bun on each of 4 plates. Spoon Sloppy Joe mixture over each. Serve, with the potato salad and cole slaw as accompaniments.

2. When ready for dessert, serve the S'mores, with milk, if desired.

Vegetarian Sloppy Joes on Whole Wheat Buns
Single serving is 1/4 of the total recipe
CALORIES 411; PROTEIN 34g; CARBS 59g;
TOTAL FAT 5g; SAT FAT 1g; CHOLESTEROL 0mg;
SODIUM 1267mg; FIBER 7g

minute

chapter 5

pasta and grain
menus

pasta in creamy artichoke and parmesan sauce

carrot salad with scallions and ripe olives

italian ices and nut biscotti

shopping list

Spinach or regular linguine or capellini

Canned artichoke hearts

Fresh flat-leaf parsley

Baby carrots

Chopped scallions (from the salad bar)

Canned sliced ripe California olives

Italian ices

Nut biscotti

from your pantry

Salt and pepper

Garlic

Butter

Grated Parmesan cheese

Dried red pepper flakes

Extra virgin olive oil

Red wine vinegar

menu
gameplan

serves 4 to 6

beforeyoustart

Bring 4 quarts of water to a boil in a large pot, covered, over high heat to cook the pasta.

step **1** make the **pasta**

step **2** assemble the **carrot salad with scallions and ripe olives**

step **3** **serve**

luckyforyou Canned artichokes are key in keeping the sauce quick to make. If you use frozen artichokes, always an option, you will need to thaw them first and cook them longer than canned artichokes, both of which will add to the time "bottom line."

"This is an easy dish to make, but it's special. Artichokes do that—to almost any dish."

—minutemeals' Chef Nancy

make the **pasta in creamy artichoke and parmesan sauce**

For the pasta

4 quarts water

Salt to taste

1 pound spinach or regular linguine or capellini

For the sauce

3 garlic cloves

1 can (14 ounces) artichoke hearts

$1/4$ cup chopped flat-leaf parsley

3 tablespoons olive oil

3 tablespoons butter

1 cup grated Parmesan cheese (about 3 ounces)

Dried red pepper flakes to taste

Salt and pepper to taste

1. Cook the pasta: Pour the water into a large pot, salt light, and cover. Bring to a boil over high heat. Add the pasta, stir to separate, and cook until *al dente*. Remove $1/2$ cup of the pasta cooking water and drain the pasta.

2. Make the sauce: Finely chop the garlic. Drain, rinse, and quarter the artichokes. Chop enough parsley to measure $1/4$ cup.

3. In the pasta cooking pot, heat the olive oil and butter over medium heat until the butter is melted. Stir in the garlic and then the artichoke hearts and parsley. Cook, stirring, until heated through, about 2 minutes. Remove the pan from the heat. Add the pasta, Parmesan, dried red pepper flakes, salt, and pepper. Toss, adding enough of the reserved pasta cooking water to make a creamy, not sticky, sauce. Cover and keep warm.

assemble the **carrot salad with scallions and ripe olives**

1 bag (16 ounces) baby carrots

$1/4$ cup chopped scallions

2 tablespoons canned sliced ripe California olives

2 tablespoons extra virgin olive oil

1 tablespoon red wine vinegar

Salt and pepper to taste

1. Bring $1/2$ inch of water to a boil, covered, in a large skillet over high heat. Add the carrots, cover, and cook until tender, about 5 minutes. Drain and transfer to a salad bowl.

2. Add the scallions, olives, oil, vinegar, and salt and pepper. Toss to coat. Place the bowl and 4 salad plates on the table.

serve

1. Divide the pasta among 4 pasta bowls, making sure that the artichoke pieces are distributed evenly. Serve, with the salad as an accompaniment.

2. When ready for dessert, scoop the Italian ice into dessert bowls and serve with or garnish with the biscotti.

Pasta in Creamy Artichoke and Parmesan Sauce
Single serving is $1/4$ of the total recipe
CALORIES 492; PROTEIN 18g; CARBS 60g;
TOTAL FAT 19g; SAT FAT 7g; CHOLESTEROL 26mg;
SODIUM 443mg; FIBER 0g

pasta and vegetables
with sesame sauce
cucumber salad with rice vinegar and scallions
banana ice cream with chocolate sauce

shopping list

Thin spaghetti

Frozen French-cut string beans

Lime

Cilantro

Kirby cucumbers

Radishes

Banana ice cream

Peanuts

from the salad bar

Broccoli florets (or from the produce department)

Shredded carrots (or from the produce department)

Chopped scallions

from your pantry

Salt and pepper

Peanut butter

Lite soy sauce

Toasted sesame oil

Garlic

Hot pepper sauce

Rice vinegar

Canola oil

Sugar

Ground ginger

Chocolate syrup

serves 4

beforeyoustart

Bring a large pot of water, covered, to a boil over high heat to cook the pasta.

step 1 make the **pasta and vegetables with sesame sauce**

step 2 assemble the **cucumber salad**

step 3 **serve**

luckyforyou You need 1 pot only to cook the pasta and vegetables, and only the food processor (or blender) to make the sauce.

"This dish is kind to the cook. The sauce can be made ahead and frozen. Thaw for 2 minutes in the microwave." —minutemeals' Chef Amanda

make the **pasta and vegetables with sesame sauce**

For the pasta and vegetables

4 quarts water

Salt to taste

12 ounces thin spaghetti

2 cups small broccoli florets

1 package (10 ounces) frozen French-cut string beans

1 cup pre-shredded carrots

For the sauce

1/2 cup peanut butter

2 tablespoons lime juice (1 large lime)

2 tablespoons lite soy sauce

2 teaspoons toasted sesame oil

2 garlic cloves

2 to 6 drops hot pepper sauce

1/3 cup cilantro sprigs

1. Cook the pasta: Pour the water into a large pot, salt lightly, and cover. Bring to a boil over high heat. Add the spaghetti, stir to separate, and cook for 5 minutes. Add the broccoli and cook for 3 minutes. Stir in the string beans and carrots and cook for 2 minutes, or until the spaghetti is *al dente*. Remove

1/3 cup of the pasta cooking water and drain the pasta and vegetables well. Return to the pot.

2. While the pasta cooks, make the sauce: In a food processor or blender, process the peanut butter, lime juice, soy sauce, sesame oil, garlic, and hot pepper sauce until smooth. Add the reserved pasta cooking water and the cilantro and process until mixed and the cilantro is chopped.

assemble the **cucumber salad with rice vinegar and scallions**

4 Kirby cucumbers

4 radishes

3 tablespoons rice vinegar

2 tablespoons canola oil

1 1/2 teaspoons sugar

Large pinch of ground ginger

2 tablespoons chopped scallions

Salt and pepper to taste

Thinly slice the cucumbers and radishes. Combine them in a serving bowl and add the remaining ingredients, tossing well to dissolve the sugar. Place the bowl on the table with 4 salad plates.

serve

1. Add the sesame sauce to the pasta and vegetables and toss well to combine. Divide among 4 pasta bowls and serve, with the salad as an accompaniment.

2. When ready for dessert, scoop the ice cream into 4 dessert bowls, top with chocolate syrup, and garnish with peanuts. Serve, with additional chocolate syrup, if desired.

Pasta and Vegetables with Sesame Sauce
Single serving is 1/4 of the total recipe
CALORIES 579; PROTEIN 21g; CARBS 78g; TOTAL FAT 21g; SAT FAT 4g; CHOLESTEROL 0mg; SODIUM 428mg; FIBER 5g

⭐ fettuccine alfredo

roasted peppers, marinated artichokes, and olives
semolina bread
oranges with grand marnier and chocolate cookies

shopping list

Navel oranges

Grand Marnier

Black and green olives

Parmesan cheese in a wedge

Semolina bread

Fettuccine, fresh or dried

Evaporated skimmed milk

Nonfat sour cream

Chocolate cookies

from the salad bar

Roasted peppers

Marinated artichokes

from your pantry

Olive oil

Salt

Freshly ground black pepper

Grated Parmesan cheese

Butter

menu
gameplan

serves 4

beforeyoustart

Bring the water to a boil in a large pot, covered, over high heat to cook the fettuccine.

step **1** prepare the **oranges with grand marnier**

step **2** plate the **roasted peppers, artichokes, and olives**

step **3** make the **fettuccine alfredo**

step **4** **serve**

luckyforyou We've called for either fresh or dried pasta. Remember, though, that fresh pasta is much quicker-cooking than dried.

step 1

prepare the **sliced oranges with grand marnier**

4 large navel oranges

Grand Marnier to taste

On a cutting board, cut a small piece of the skin off the bottom of each orange. Holding the orange upright and starting at the top, cut the skin off each orange. Cut the oranges crosswise into thin slices. Arrange, overlapping the slices, on a shallow platter and drizzle with Grand Marnier or another orange-flavored liqueur. Refrigerate until serving time.

step 2

plate the **roasted peppers, marinated artichokes, and olives**

Roasted peppers for 4

Marinated artichokes for 4

Black and green olives

1 wedge Parmesan cheese

Olive oil for drizzling

Freshly ground black pepper

Semolina bread

1. On a serving platter, arrange the roasted peppers, artichokes, and olives. With a vegetable peeler, shave thin slices of the Parmesan and lay them across the top of the vegetables. Place the platter on the table with 4 salad plates, a small bottle of olive oil, and a pepper mill.

2. Place the semolina bread on a bread board and place on the table.

step 3

make the **fettuccine alfredo**

For the pasta

4 quarts water

Salt to taste

12 ounces fresh or dried fettuccine

For the sauce

1 cup evaporated skimmed milk

1/2 cup nonfat sour cream

1 cup grated Parmesan cheese, plus additional for serving

2 tablespoons butter

Freshly ground black pepper to taste

1. Cook the pasta: Pour the water into a large pot, salt lightly, and cover. Bring to a boil over high heat. Add the fettuccine, stir to separate the strands, and cook according to the directions on the package until just *al dente*. Drain well and return to the pot.

2. Make the sauce: In a medium saucepan, heat the evaporated milk until hot. Remove the pan from the heat and stir in the sour cream and the Parmesan until thoroughly combined. Add the butter, place the pan over low heat, and cook, stirring, until the butter is melted and the sauce has thickened slightly.

3. Pour the sauce over the pasta, toss to coat the strands, then add a generous amount of fresh black pepper. Toss to combine.

step 4

serve

1. Serve the fettuccine immediately, in 4 pasta bowls, with additional Parmesan for serving at the table.

2. Serve the bread with both the vegetable platter and the fettuccine.

3. When ready for dessert, plate the cookies. Spoon the chilled oranges into 4 dessert bowls with any juice that has collected in the serving bowl. Serve the oranges with the cookies.

Fettuccine Alfredo
Single serving is 1/4 of the total recipe
CALORIES 532; PROTEIN 29g; CARBS 62g;
TOTAL FAT 17g; SAT FAT 6g; CHOLESTEROL 42mg;
SODIUM 571mg; FIBER 9g

☆ pasta with tomato vodka sauce

tricolor salad with walnuts

focaccia with olive oil for dipping

long-stemmed sugared strawberries

menu
gameplan

shopping list

Thin spaghetti

Heavy cream

Tomato paste

Diced tomatoes
(from the salad bar)

Fresh basil

Prewashed Italian-style
salad mix

Belgian endive

Walnut pieces

Focaccia

Long-stemmed strawberries

from your pantry

Salt and pepper

Garlic

Vodka

Dried red pepper flakes

Grated Parmesan cheese

Olive oil

Balsamic vinegar

Dijon mustard

Confectioners' sugar

serves 4

beforeyoustart

Bring the water to a boil in a large pot, covered, over high heat to cook the pasta. Rinse the strawberries and let drain.

step	1	cook the **pasta with tomato vodka sauce**
step	2	assemble the **tricolor salad with walnuts**
step	3	plate the **focaccia with olive oil for dipping**
step	4	**serve**

headsup

When you drain the tomatoes, reserve some of the liquid, just in case the sauce needs thinning.

"This great-tasting sauce cooks up in less time than it takes to cook the pasta. Try it with penne or fusilli, too."

—minutemeals' Chef Paul

step 1

cook the **pasta with tomato vodka sauce**

For the pasta

4 quarts water

Salt to taste

1 pound thin spaghetti

For the sauce

2 large garlic cloves

1/4 cup vodka

1/2 cup heavy cream

3 tablespoons tomato paste

1/4 teaspoon dried red pepper flakes

1 can (15 ounces) diced tomatoes (drained, but with some liquid reserved)

1/4 cup grated Parmesan cheese plus additional for serving

1/4 cup fresh basil leaves

1. Cook the pasta: Pour the water into a large pot, salt lightly, and cover. Bring to a boil over high heat. Add the pasta, stir to separate, and cook according to the directions on the package until just *al dente*. Drain well.

2. Make the sauce: Flatten the garlic with the broad side of a knife. Place the garlic in a large saucepan with the vodka and bring to boil, covered, over high heat. Boil for 1 minute. Add the cream, tomato paste, and red pepper flakes and bring to a boil, covered. Reduce the heat and simmer for 4 minutes. Remove and discard the garlic.

3. Drain the tomatoes.

4. Stir the tomatoes and Parmesan into the sauce and cook for 1 to 2 minutes, or until heated through. If desired, thin the sauce to taste with a small amount of the reserved tomato liquid.

step 2

assemble the **tricolor salad with walnuts**

1 garlic clove

1/4 cup olive oil

2 tablespoons balsamic vinegar

2 teaspoons Dijon mustard

Salt and pepper to taste

1 bag (5 to 7 ounces) pre-washed Italian-style salad mix

1 small Belgian endive

1/4 cup walnut pieces

1. Peel and cut the garlic and rub the cut halves over the surface of a salad bowl. Add the oil, vinegar, and mustard. Whisk with a fork until blended. Season with salt and pepper.

2. Place the salad greens over the dressing. Cut the endive into 1-inch pieces and add to the bowl. Sprinkle with the walnuts. Place the bowl on the table with 4 salad plates.

step 3

plate the **focaccia with olive oil for dipping**

1 store-bought focaccia

Olive oil for dipping

1. Place the focaccia on a bread board.

2. Pour olive oil into a small shallow bowl. Place the bread and oil on the table.

step 4

serve

1. Finish the pasta: Cut the basil leaves into thin slivers. Add the vodka sauce to the pasta and toss well to combine. Add half of the basil, spoon onto a serving platter, and garnish with the remaining basil. Place the platter on the table with 4 pasta bowls. Serve with additional grated Parmesan on the side.

2. Toss the salad at the table and serve with the pasta and bread and oil.

3. When ready for dessert, place the strawberries in a shallow serving bowl. Dust with confectioners' sugar or place the sugar in a bowl and pass at the table. Serve the berries, with dessert plates.

Pasta with Tomato Vodka Sauce
Single serving is 1/4 of the total recipe
CALORIES 563; PROTEIN 29g; CARBS 80g;
TOTAL FAT 10g; SAT FAT 5g; CHOLESTEROL 25mg;
SODIUM 156mg; FIBER 4g

spinach pasta with asian dressing

miso soup with crispy chinese noodles

sliced bananas with berry yogurt

shopping list

Spinach pasta

Frozen edamame
(green soybeans)

Ginger

1 can vegetable broth

Firm tofu

Mellow white miso

Crispy Chinese noodles

Ripe bananas

Mixed berry yogurt

from the salad bar

Pretrimmed mixed cauliflower
and broccoli florets (or from
the produce department)

Sliced scallions

from your pantry

Salt and pepper

Rice vinegar

Toasted sesame oil

Canola oil

Lite soy sauce

Honey

serves 4

beforeyoustart

Bring the water to a boil in a large
pot, covered, over high heat to cook
the pasta.

step	1	cook the **spinach pasta**
step	2	prepare the **miso soup with crispy chinese noodles**
step	3	prepare the **sliced bananas with berry yogurt**
step	4	serve

luckyforyou Many supermarkets now
stock combined cauliflower
and broccoli florets in bags in the produce department.
The fact that they are ready to use impacts greatly on the
preparation time of a pasta dish like this. If they're not
available, omit the cauliflower entirely, buy broccoli crowns,
and trim them yourself.

"If you have leftovers, they make a tasty chilled pasta salad the next day."

—minutemeals' Chef Ruth

step 1

cook the **spinach pasta with asian dressing**

For the pasta

3 quarts water

Salt to taste

8 ounces strand spinach pasta

1 bag (12 ounces) pretrimmed mixed small cauliflower and broccoli florets

2 cups frozen edamame (green soybeans)

For the dressing

2-inch piece of fresh ginger, grated (about 1 tablespoon)

3 tablespoons rice vinegar

2 tablespoons toasted sesame oil

2 tablespoons canola oil

2 tablespoons lite soy sauce

2 tablespoons honey

Salt and pepper to taste

1. Cook the pasta: Pour the water into a large pot, salt lightly, and cover. Bring to a boil over high heat. Add the pasta, stir to separate, and cook according to the directions on the package. About 6 minutes before the pasta is due to be finished, add the cauliflower and broccoli florets and edamame to the pot and continue boiling until the pasta is cooked *al dente*, the florets are just tender, and the edamame are heated through. Drain well.

2. While the pasta is cooking, make the dressing: Peel and grate the ginger.

3. In a medium bowl, with a fork, whisk together the rice vinegar, sesame oil, canola oil, soy sauce, and honey. Stir in the ginger. Season with salt and pepper.

4. Transfer the pasta and vegetables to a serving bowl, pour the dressing over the top, and toss to combine.

step 2

prepare the **miso soup with crispy chinese noodles**

1 can (14 1/2 ounces) vegetable broth

4 ounces firm tofu

1/4 cup sliced scallions

2 tablespoons mellow white miso

1 package crispy Chinese noodles

1. In a saucepan, bring the vegetable broth to a simmer.

2. While the soup heats, dice the tofu. Add the tofu and the scallions to the broth and simmer 30 seconds.

3. Remove the broth from the heat and stir in the miso.

step 3

prepare the **sliced bananas with berry yogurt**

4 large ripe bananas

1 container (8 ounces) mixed berry yogurt

1. Slice the bananas, dividing them among 4 dessert bowls.

2. Stir the yogurt until smooth, then spoon some of it over the bananas in each bowl. Stir to combine and refrigerate until dessert time.

step 4

serve

1. Serve the soup in small bowls, either with the Chinese noodles on top, or as an accompaniment.

2. Serve the pasta and vegetables in pasta bowls.

3. When ready for dessert, serve the bananas with yogurt.

Spinach Pasta with Asian Dressing
Single serving is 1/4 of the total recipe
CALORIES 508; PROTEIN 19g; CARBS 62g;
TOTAL FAT 21g; SAT FAT 3g; CHOLESTEROL 0mg;
SODIUM 312mg; FIBER 5g

quick thai noodles
mango and pineapple salad
coconut ice cream

shopping list

Thin egg noodles, preferably Chinese style

Limes (for juice)

Fish sauce or lite soy sauce

Fresh bean sprouts

Cilantro

Thai red curry paste or chile paste

Pre-shredded cole slaw mix (bagged, from the produce department)

Dry-roasted peanuts

Ripe mangoes

Canned pineapple chunks, packed in juice

Coconut ice cream

from your pantry

Salt

Maple syrup

Vegetable oil

Ground cinnamon

serves 6

beforeyoustart
Bring the water to a boil in a large pot, covered, over high heat to cook the noodles.

step 1 make the **quick thai noodles**

step 2 assemble the **mango and pineapple salad**

step 3 **serve**

luckyforyou Ready-to-serve cole slaw mix, bagged in the produce department, keeps prep time for this popular noodle dish (and cleanup time) to the absolute minimum.

"Want to boost the protein in this dish? Add a pound of baked tofu, diced, in the last few minutes of cooking."

—minutemeals' Chef Nancy

make the **quick thai noodles**

For the pasta

4 quarts water

Salt to taste

1 pound thin egg noodles, preferably Chinese style

For the sauce

2 or 3 large limes
(enough for 1/4 cup juice)

2 tablespoons fish sauce or soy sauce

2 tablespoons maple syrup

1/2 pound fresh bean sprouts

1/2 cup packed coarsely chopped cilantro

3 tablespoons vegetable oil

1 tablespoon Thai red curry paste or chile paste

4 cups pre-shredded cole slaw mix with cabbage and carrots

1 1/2 cups dry-roasted peanuts

1. Cook the pasta: Pour the water into a large pot, salt lightly, and cover. Bring to a boil over high heat. Add the noodles, stir to separate, and cook according to the directions on the package until *al dente*. Drain and rinse briefly under cold running water. Transfer to a large serving bowl.

2. Make the vegetables and sauce: In a small bowl, stir together the lime juice, fish sauce, and maple syrup.

3. Rinse and drain the bean sprouts. Coarsely chop enough cilantro to measure 1/2 cup.

4. Heat the vegetable oil in a wok or a deep 12-inch skillet over high heat until hot. Add the curry or chile paste. Cook, stirring, for a few seconds. Add the cole slaw mix. Cook, tossing, until the vegetables are slightly softened, about 3 minutes. Toss frequently, scraping the curry or chili paste off the bottom of the pan to prevent it from burning.

5. Add the bean sprouts to the pan and cook, stirring, just until heated, about 2 minutes. Pour in the lime juice mixture and stir to coat evenly. Remove the pan from the heat. Add the vegetables to the noodles and toss to combine.

6. Add half of the cilantro and half of the peanuts to the bowl and toss well. Sprinkle with the remaining peanuts and cilantro.

assemble the **mango and pineapple salad**

2 ripe mangoes

1 cup canned pineapple chunks packed in juice, drained

2 to 3 teaspoons fresh lime juice

1/4 teaspoon ground cinnamon

1. With a vegetable peeler, peel the mangoes. With a sharp knife, cut the fruit off the pits and cut it into chunks. Place the mango in a salad bowl.

2. Add the pineapple. Sprinkle with the lime juice and cinnamon and toss gently to coat. Place the bowl on the table with 6 salad plates.

serve

1. Place the platter of noodles on the table. Serve on 6 dinner plates, with the fruit salad as an accompaniment.

2. When ready for dessert, scoop the ice cream into 6 small dessert bowls. Serve.

Quick Thai Noodles
Single serving is 1/6 of the total recipe
CALORIES 409; PROTEIN 16g; CARBS 33g;
TOTAL FAT 26g; SAT FAT 4g; CHOLESTEROL 25mg;
SODIUM 211mg; FIBER 7g

penne in cream sauce
with vegetables
greens with fresh fruit
crusty black olive bread
chocolate gelato
with mango sorbet

menu gameplan

shopping list

Penne

Green beans

Broccoli florets
(from the salad bar or from
the produce department)

Canned whole tomatoes

Fresh basil

Fat-free sour cream

Arugula or prewashed spring
greens or baby spinach

Ripe peaches, nectarines,
or raspberries

Crusty black olive bread

Chocolate gelato

Mango sorbet

from your pantry

Onion

Garlic

Skim milk

Grated Parmesan cheese

Ground nutmeg

Extra virgin olive oil

Balsamic vinegar

Freshly ground black pepper

serves 4

beforeyoustart
Bring the water in a large pot to a
boil, covered, over high heat to cook
the pasta.

step	1	cook the **penne in cream sauce with vegetables**
step	2	assemble the **salad**
step	3	**serve**

headsup

The balsamic vinegar that we are suggesting you use on the salads is the expensive variety typically sold at gourmet food shops. It should be used sparingly as it has been aged, just like fine wine. If you don't have balsamic vinegar like that, omit it entirely and dress the greens with red wine vinaigrette, either homemade or store-bought.

step 1

cook the **penne in cream sauce with vegetables**

For the pasta

3 quarts water

8 ounces penne

1 pound fresh green beans

8 ounces broccoli florets

For the sauce

1 small onion

2 cloves garlic

1 can (28 ounces) whole tomatoes

2 tablespoons fresh basil

2 teaspoons olive oil

1/2 cup fat-free sour cream

2 tablespoons skim milk

1/4 cup grated Parmesan cheese

Pinch ground nutmeg

1. Cook the pasta: Pour the water into a large pot, cover, and bring to a boil over high heat. Add the penne, stir to separate, and cook according to the directions on the package until barely *al dente*.

2. Meanwhile, slice the green beans in half. Add the green beans and the broccoli florets to the pasta for the last 3 minutes of cooking time. Drain the pasta and vegetables well and return to the pot.

3. Make the sauce: Chop the onion and the garlic. Drain the tomatoes and chop coarsely. Slice or tear enough fresh basil to measure 2 tablespoons.

4. In a large nonstick skillet, heat the olive oil over medium heat until hot. Add the onion and garlic and cook, stirring, until the onion is softened, about 3 minutes. Add the tomatoes and cook, stirring occasionally, until hot, about 4 minutes.

5. Remove the skillet from the heat and stir in the sour cream, skim milk, Parmesan, basil, and nutmeg until combined. Pour the cream sauce over the penne and toss thoroughly to coat and combine. Keep warm, covered.

step 2

assemble the **greens with fresh fruit**

8 ounces arugula, or prewashed spring greens or baby spinach

2 teaspoons extra virgin olive oil

2 ripe peaches or nectarines, or 1/2 pint fresh raspberries

Balsamic vinegar for serving

Freshly ground black pepper to taste

1. If using arugula, remove the stems, wash the leaves, and spin dry.

2. In a large bowl, toss the greens with the olive oil. Divide the greens among 4 salad plates. If using peaches or nectarines, slice each into 8 pieces. Arrange the slices or the raspberries on the greens.

step 3

serve

1. Divide the penne and vegetables among 4 pasta bowls and serve.

2. Place the salads on the table, with the balsamic vinegar for drizzling over the top. Pass a pepper mill at the table for grinding over the fruit.

3. Place the bread on a bread board and serve with the pasta and salads.

4. When ready for dessert, scoop the chocolate gelato into 4 dessert bowls, and garnish each serving with a spoonful or two of the sorbet. Serve.

Penne in Cream Sauce with Vegetables
Single serving is 1/4 of the total recipe
CALORIES 388; PROTEIN 17g; CARBS 69g;
TOTAL FAT 8g; SAT FAT 2g; CHOLESTEROL 6mg;
SODIUM 1127mg; FIBER 3g

macaroni with broccoli rabe

antipasto

parmesan toasts

blueberries with orange sherbet

serves 4

shopping list

Macaroni

Broccoli rabe

Jarred marinated artichoke hearts

Jarred roasted red peppers

Jarred pepperoncini

Olives

Semolina bread

Blueberries, fresh or quick-thaw frozen

Orange sherbet

from your pantry

Salt

Garlic

Extra virgin olive oil

Dried red pepper flakes

Grated Parmesan cheese

beforeyoustart

Bring a large pot of water to a boil, covered, over high heat.

step	1	make the **macaroni with broccoli rabe**
step	2	prepare the **antipasto**
step	3	make the **parmesan toasts**
step	4	prepare the **blueberries with orange sherbet**
step	5	**serve**

 **headsup** Remember that the stems of broccoli rabe will take longer to cook than the leaves. It's a good idea, therefore, to add the stems to the skillet first, to allow them a little extra cooking time. Otherwise they can be crisp to the point of being chewy.

"Eight cloves of garlic may seem like an enormous amount, but it's really not because garlic mellows as it cooks in the oil."

—minutemeals' Chef Miriam

step 1

make the **macaroni with broccoli rabe**

4 quarts water

Salt to taste

1 box (16 ounces) macaroni

1 bunch broccoli rabe
(about 1¼ pounds)

6 to 8 garlic cloves

⅓ cup extra virgin olive oil

¼ teaspoon dried red pepper
flakes

Grated Parmesan cheese
for serving (optional)

1. Pour the water into a large pot, salt lightly, and cover. Bring to a boil over high heat. Add the macaroni, stir to separate, and cook according to the directions on the package, stirring occasionally, until tender. Remove and reserve ½ cup of the pasta cooking liquid. Drain the macaroni well and return to the pot.

2. Cut the tough stems off the broccoli rabe, then cut it into 1½-inch pieces. Slice the garlic.

3. In a large deep skillet, heat the olive oil over medium heat until warm. Add the garlic and red pepper flakes and cook, stirring occasionally, until the garlic is golden, about 3 minutes.

4. Add the broccoli rabe and cook over medium-high heat, stirring occasionally, about 3 or 4 minutes, until tender. Remove the pan from the heat and keep warm, covered.

step 2

prepare the **antipasto**

Jarred marinated artichoke
hearts

Jarred roasted peppers

Jarred pepperoncini

A selection of green and black
olives

Drain each of the antipasto selections, then arrange on a large platter. Place the platter on the table with 4 salad plates.

step 3

make the **parmesan toasts**

1 loaf semolina bread

Extra virgin olive oil for brushing

Grated Parmesan cheese
as needed

1. Preheat the broiler.

2. Cut the semolina loaf into ½-inch-thick slices. Brush the slices on both sides with extra virgin olive oil and place on a baking sheet. Broil about 4 inches from the heat until golden, about 1 minute. Turn and broil the second side until golden.

3. Sprinkle the rounds with Parmesan and broil for 1 minute, or until the cheese is melted. Place on a serving plate.

step 4

prepare the **blueberries with orange sherbet**

Fresh or thawed quick-thaw
frozen blueberries

1 pint orange sherbet

1. If using fresh blueberries, pick them over and rinse in a colander. Let stand until serving time. If using frozen berries, thaw them according to the directions on the package.

2. Remove the sherbet from the freezer to soften before serving.

step 5

serve

1. Add the broccoli rabe mixture and the reserved ½ cup pasta cooking liquid to the macaroni and toss well to combine. Season with salt, if desired. Cover and keep warm while having the antipasto platter with the Parmesan toasts.

2. Divide the macaroni and broccoli rabe among 4 pasta bowls or plates. Serve, with additional grated Parmesan, if desired.

3. When ready for dessert, scoop orange sherbet into 4 dessert bowls and scatter blueberries over the top. Serve, with the remaining blueberries, if desired.

Macaroni with Broccoli Rabe
Single serving is ¼ of the total recipe

CALORIES 366; PROTEIN 10g; CARBS 41g;
TOTAL FAT 19g; SAT FAT 3g; CHOLESTEROL 0mg;
SODIUM 78mg; FIBER 3g

pasta with potatoes, green beans, and pesto

mozzarella cheese and olives

breadsticks

apricots with amaretti

serves 4

shopping list

Macaroni or other small tubular pasta

Frozen cut green beans

Red-skinned potatoes

Prepared pesto

Fresh mozzarella, or mild Gouda cheese

Sweet or red onion slices (optional) (from the salad bar)

Green or ripe olives (jarred or from the salad bar)

Italian dressing

Breadsticks

Canned apricots packed in syrup (a 16-ounce can)

Amaretti

from your pantry

Salt

Shredded Parmesan cheese

beforeyoustart

Bring the water to a boil in a large pot, covered, over high heat to cook the pasta.

step 1 make the **pasta with potatoes, green beans, and pesto**

step 2 plate the **mozzarella cheese and olives**

step 3 serve

luckyforyou The potatoes, which can take a while when cooked stovetop, cook in the microwave oven in this recipe in all of 6 minutes.

"Strand pasta with potatoes, green beans, and pesto is a classic dish in the North of Italy, and this delicious version takes only 20 minutes."

—minutemeals' Chef Ruth

step 1

make the **pasta with potatoes, green beans, and pesto**

3 quarts water

Salt to taste

8 ounces macaroni or other small tubular pasta

1 package (8 to 9 ounces) frozen cut green beans

12 ounces small red-skinned potatoes

1/2 cup prepared pesto sauce

3/4 cup shredded Parmesan cheese

1. Pour the water into a large pot, salt lightly, and cover. Bring the water to a boil over high heat. Add the macaroni, stir to separate, and cook according to the directions on the package until *al dente*. About 3 minutes before the pasta is finished, add the green beans to the pot and cook until just tender. Remove 1/2 cup of the pasta cooking water and reserve. Drain the pasta and beans well, return to the pot, and keep warm, covered.

2. While the pasta and beans are cooking, scrub the potatoes and cut them into 1/2-inch cubes. Place the cubes in a microwave-safe dish, add 1 tablespoon water, and cover. Microwave on High about 6 minutes, stirring once, until fork-tender.

step 2

plate the **mozzarella cheese and olives**

Fresh mozzarella (or mild Gouda cheese)

Sweet or red onion slices (optional)

Green and ripe olives of choice

2 tablespoons prepared Italian dressing

1. Slice the mozzarella into as thin slices as possible and arrange around the outside rim of a platter.

2. Place the onion slices, if using, in the center of the platter, and scatter the olives over them. Drizzle the antipasto with the dressing and place the platter on the table with 4 salad plates.

step 3

serve

1. Transfer the pasta and green beans to a large serving bowl. Drain the potatoes and add to the bowl. Drop spoonfuls of the pesto over the pasta and vegetables and toss lightly, adding the reserved pasta cooking water if the mixture is too thick. Sprinkle with the shredded Parmesan cheese. Ladle the pasta at once into 4 large pasta bowls and serve.

2. Serve the mozzarella and olives as an accompaniment or as a starter with the breadsticks.

3. When ready for dessert, serve the apricots with some of their syrup in 4 dessert bowls with the amaretti as an accompaniment, or crumble them over the fruit.

Pasta with Potatoes, Green Beans, and Pesto
Single serving is 1/4 of the total recipe

CALORIES 493; PROTEIN 18g; CARBS 65g;
TOTAL FAT 19g; SAT FAT 6g; CHOLESTEROL 19g;
SODIUM 498g; FIBER 3g

mini ravioli
with pesto and cherry tomatoes

grilled portobello mushrooms

semolina bread

fresh peaches or crisp apples

shopping list

Fresh or frozen mini cheese ravioli

Cherry tomatoes (from the salad bar)

Fresh basil

Walnuts or pine nuts

Portobello mushrooms

Quality balsamic vinaigrette

Semolina bread

Ripe peaches or apples

from your pantry

Salt and pepper

Garlic

Extra virgin olive oil

Grated Parmesan cheese

serves 4

beforeyoustart

Bring a large pot of water to a boil, covered, over high heat to cook the pasta.

step **1** make the **mini ravioli**

step **2** prepare the **grilled portobello mushrooms**

step **3** **serve**

 Although purists believe that pesto should only be made by hand with a mortar and pestle, we think this food processor or blender version tastes just fine. And it's quick.

"If you don't mind the calories, add a tablespoon of softened butter to the pesto to help the sauce cling to the pasta."

—minutemeals' Chef Paul

make the **mini ravioli with pesto and cherry tomatoes**

For the pasta

4 quarts water

Salt to taste

1 pound (16 ounces) fresh or frozen mini cheese ravioli

2 cups cherry tomatoes

For the pesto

2 cups packed fresh basil leaves

1 garlic clove, peeled

3 tablespoons walnuts or pine nuts

3 tablespoons extra virgin olive oil

4 tablespoons grated Parmesan cheese, plus additional for serving

Salt and pepper to taste

1. Cook the pasta: Pour the water into a large pot, salt lightly, and cover. Bring to a boil over high heat. Add the ravioli, stir to separate, and cook according to the directions on the package. One minute before the ravioli are done, stir in the cherry tomatoes. Remove 1/2 cup of the pasta cooking water and reserve. Drain the ravioli and tomatoes and return to the pot.

2. Meanwhile, make the pesto: Place the basil, garlic, and walnuts in a food processor or blender and process until finely chopped. With the machine running, pour in the olive oil and process until smooth. Add the Parmesan and process until combined. Season with salt and pepper.

prepare the **grilled portobello mushrooms**

4 portobello mushrooms

1/4 cup store-bought balsamic vinaigrette

Salt and pepper to taste

1. Preheat a grill pan or large skillet over medium heat. Remove the stems on the mushrooms and discard. Wipe the mushroom caps clean with paper towels.

2. Brush the tops of the mushroom caps with some of the vinaigrette and place, brushed side down, on the grill pan or in the skillet. Grill for 6 to 8 minutes, turning halfway during the cooking and brushing with remaining vinaigrette. Transfer the mushrooms to a cutting board and cut them into 1-inch strips. Season with salt and pepper.

serve

1. Add the pesto to the ravioli and cherry tomatoes, with some of the reserved pasta cooking liquid to thin the sauce to the desired consistency. Toss well to combine, then ladle into 4 pasta bowls and serve with additional grated Parmesan at the table.

2. Serve the grilled portobello strips on separate small plates with the pasta.

3. When ready for dessert, serve the fruit on 4 dessert plates, with knives for cutting it into slices.

Mini Ravioli with Pesto and Cherry Tomatoes
Single serving is 1/4 of the total recipe
CALORIES 527; PROTEIN 16g; CARBS 37g;
TOTAL FAT 24g; SAT FAT 6g; CHOLESTEROL 69mg;
SODIUM 312mg; FIBER 2g

spicy couscous
with squash, almonds, and cranberries

italian greens with gorgonzola vinaigrette
onion pita bread
plums with sour cream

menu gameplan

serves 4

beforeyoustart
Place plums in the refrigerator to chill.

step	1	make the **couscous**
step	2	while the **couscous** stands, assemble the **salad**
step	3	**serve**

shopping list

Frozen cubed butternut squash

Scallions

Slivered almonds

Dried cranberries

Couscous

Crumbled Gorgonzola cheese

Prewashed Italian-style salad greens

Sliced celery (from the salad bar)

Onion pita breads

Canned plums packed in heavy syrup (1 16-ounce can)

Light sour cream

from your pantry

Vegetable broth

Butter

Honey

Curry powder

Cayenne pepper

Extra virgin olive oil

White wine vinegar

Dijon mustard

Salt and pepper

headsup
Look for frozen squash cubes packed in plastic bags, weighing approximately 1 pound, in the freezer section of the supermarket.

"If you have leftover crumbled gorgonzola, serve it with ripe pears and toasted pecans for dessert or for a snack during the week."

—minutemeals' Chef Paul

step 1

make the **spicy couscous with squash, almonds, and cranberries**

1 can (14 1/2 ounces) vegetable broth

2 tablespoons butter

1 tablespoon honey

1 teaspoon ground curry powder

1/8 teaspoon cayenne pepper

1 bag (16 ounces) frozen cubed butternut squash

4 scallions

1/3 cup slivered almonds

1/3 cup dried cranberries

1 1/4 cups couscous

1. In a large saucepan, combine the broth, butter, honey, curry powder, cayenne, and squash. Cover and bring to a boil over high heat. Reduce the heat to low and cook for 3 to 4 minutes, or until the squash is just tender.

2. Slice the scallions.

3. Place the almonds on a paper towel and microwave on High for 50 to 70 seconds, or until fragrant.

4. Stir the scallions, cranberries, and couscous into the squash mixture. Cover and remove the pan from the heat. Let stand for 5 minutes.

step 2

while the **couscous** stands, assemble the **italian greens with gorgonzola vinaigrette**

1/4 cup extra virgin olive oil

1 1/2 tablespoons white wine vinegar

1 teaspoon Dijon mustard

2 tablespoons crumbled Gorgonzola cheese, plus additional for serving

Salt and pepper to taste

1 cup sliced celery

1 bag (5 to 7 ounces) prewashed Italian-style salad greens

1. In a salad bowl, whisk together the olive oil, wine vinegar, mustard, and Gorgonzola until blended. Season with salt and pepper.

2. Place the celery in the bowl and top with the salad greens. Place the bowl on the table.

step 3

serve

1. Add about half the almonds to the couscous mixture and stir gently with a serving spoon to distribute them. Spoon the couscous into a serving bowl and sprinkle the remaining almonds on top. Serve immediately, with the onion pita breads as an accompaniment.

2. Toss the salad and serve with additional Gorgonzola, if desired.

3. When ready for dessert, divide the plums and some of their syrup among 4 dessert bowls, and top, if desired, with a dollop of sour cream. Serve, with additional sour cream.

Spicy Couscous with Squash, Almonds, and Cranberries
Single serving is 1/4 of the total recipe

CALORIES 445; PROTEIN 11g; CARBS 75g; TOTAL FAT 13g; SAT FAT 4g; CHOLESTEROL 16mg; SODIUM 104mg; FIBER 5g

bulghur
with currants, chickpeas, and zucchini
sliced tomatoes with garlic-and-herbed cheese
orange and raspberry sorbet

menu gameplan

serves 4

| step | 1 | make the **bulghur** |

| step | 2 | plate the **sliced tomatoes** |

| step | 3 | **serve** |

shopping list

Bulghur

Dried currants or raisins

Caribbean spice blend

Zucchini

Chickpeas

Chopped onions
(from the salad bar)

Lemon

Vine-ripe tomatoes

Quality balsamic vinaigrette

Garlic-and-herb cheese
spread, such as Boursin

Orange sorbet

Raspberry sorbet

from your pantry

Honey

Salt

luckyforyou Spice companies are now making spice blends to save time as well as money. To sidestep buying the Caribbean blend, combine ½ teaspoon each of ground cumin and chili powder and ⅛ teaspoon each of ground cinnamon and cayenne pepper.

"The popular Middle Eastern salad tabbouleh is made with bulghur. So if you like it, I'll wager that you'll like this dish, too."

—minutemeals' Chef Paul

step 1

make the **bulghur with currants, chickpeas, and zucchini**

- 3/4 cup medium bulghur wheat
- 1 1/2 cups water
- 1/3 cup dried currants or raisins
- 2 teaspoons honey
- 1 teaspoon Caribbean spice blend
- 3/4 teaspoon salt
- 3/4 pound small zucchini (about 3)
- 1 can (15 ounces) chickpeas
- 1/3 cup chopped onions
- 1 lemon for serving

1. In a large saucepan, stir together the bulghur, water, currants, honey, spice blend, and salt. Cover and bring to a boil over high heat.

2. Meanwhile, trim the zucchini, halve lengthwise, and slice. Rinse and drain the chickpeas.

3. Stir the zucchini into the pan. Reduce the heat to low, cover, and simmer for 5 minutes. Stir in the chickpeas and chopped onions. Remove the pan from the heat and let stand, still covered, for 10 minutes.

step 2

plate the **sliced tomatoes with garlic-and-herbed cheese**

- 5 medium vine-ripe tomatoes
- 2 tablespoons quality balsamic vinaigrette
- 1 package (5.2 ounces) garlic-and-herb cheese spread, such as Boursin

1. Rinse the tomatoes, pat dry, and thinly slice. Arrange the slices on a serving plate and drizzle with the vinaigrette.

2. Crumble the cheese over the tomatoes. Place the plate on the table with 4 salad plates.

step 3

serve

1. Fluff the bulghur mixture with a fork. Cut the lemon into wedges. Spoon the bulghur mixture onto 4 dinner plates and place a lemon wedge or 2 on each. Serve at once, with the salad as an accompaniment.

2. When ready for dessert, scoop both sorbets into 4 dessert bowls. Serve.

Bulghur with Currants, Chickpeas, and Zucchini
Single serving is 1/4 of the total recipe
CALORIES 259; PROTEIN 9g; CARBS 53g;
TOTAL FAT 2g; SAT FAT 0g; CHOLESTEROL 0mg;
SODIUM 564mg; FIBER 7g

garden medley rice
tomato and egg salad
blueberries with lemon curd

menu
gameplan

shopping list

Frozen green peas

Ripe plum tomatoes

Prewashed salad greens
of choice

Bottled buttermilk ranch
dressing

Fresh or quick-thaw
frozen blueberries

Jarred lemon curd

from the salad bar

Assorted fresh vegetables,
such as broccoli florets,
shredded carrots, sliced
celery, chopped red pepper

Peeled hard-cooked eggs

from your pantry

Garlic

Olive oil

Frozen chopped onion,
or fresh yellow onion

Salt and pepper

Vegetable broth

Instant white rice

Fines herbes or
herbes de Provence

Shredded Parmesan cheese

serves 4

step	1	make the **garden medley rice**
step	2	assemble the **tomato and egg salad**
step	3	prepare the **blueberries with lemon curd**
step	4	**serve**

Instant rice makes this bowl
food easy to make.

step 1

make the **garden medley rice**

- 1 garlic clove
- 2 tablespoons olive oil
- 1/4 cup frozen or fresh chopped onion
- 3 cups assorted fresh vegetables, such as broccoli florets, shredded carrots, sliced celery, chopped red pepper
- 1 package (10 ounces) frozen green peas
- Salt and pepper to taste
- 3 cups vegetable broth
- 2 cups instant rice
- 2 teaspoons fines herbes or herbes de Provence
- 1/2 cup shredded Parmesan cheese, for serving

1. Mince the garlic.

2. Heat the olive oil in a large non-stick saucepan over medium heat until hot. Add the garlic and onion and cook, stirring, for 2 minutes. Add the mixed vegetables and peas and season with salt and pepper. Cook, stirring often, for 2 minutes.

3. Add the vegetable broth, cover, and bring to a boil over high heat. Reduce the heat to medium, and simmer for 5 minutes, or until the vegetables are tender.

4. Stir the rice and the herbs into the vegetable mixture until well combined. Cover the pan, remove it from the heat, and let stand 5 minutes.

step 2

assemble the **tomato and egg salad**

- 4 ripe plum tomatoes
- 4 peeled hard-cooked eggs
- 4 cups prewashed salad greens of choice
- 2 to 3 tablespoons buttermilk ranch dressing
- Salt and pepper to taste

1. Rinse the tomatoes, pat dry, and slice. Quarter each of the eggs.

2. Divide the salad greens among 4 salad plates. Top with tomato slices and wedges of egg, dividing them equally. Spoon some of the dressing over each and season with salt and pepper. Place the salads on the table.

step 3

prepare the **blueberries with lemon curd**

- 1 pint fresh or quick-thaw frozen blueberries, thawed
- 1 jar (12 ounces) jarred lemon curd

If using fresh blueberries, pick them over and rinse them. Let stand until ready to serve.

step 4

serve

1. Fluff the rice mixture with a fork and season it with salt and pepper. Transfer it to a large serving bowl and sprinkle it with the Parmesan. Place the bowl, with serving bowls, on the table.

2. Serve the salads as an accompaniment to the rice.

3. When ready for dessert, divide the blueberries among 4 dessert bowls and top each with a generous dollop of the lemon curd. Serve additional lemon curd curd at the table, if desired.

Garden Medley Rice
Single serving is 1/4 of the total recipe
CALORIES 310; PROTEIN 12g; CARBS 41g;
TOTAL FAT 12g; SAT FAT 3g; CHOLESTEROL 13mg;
SODIUM 313mg; FIBER 1g

warm lemony rice, red bean, and radish slaw
cool tomato soup
seedless watermelon wedges or green grapes

serves 4

shopping list

Scallions

Diced tomatoes with mild green chiles

Instant brown rice

Red kidney beans

Cilantro or fresh flat-leaf parsley

Lemons (for juice)

Radishes

Presliced cabbage (bagged, from the produce department)

Shredded carrots (from the salad bar or from the produce department)

Seedless watermelon or green grapes

from your pantry

Vegetable broth

Sugar

Ground cumin

Salt and pepper

Olive oil

step 1 prepare the **cool tomato soup**

step 2 make the **warm salad**

step 3 serve

 Instant brown rice cooks in only 10 minutes, about one-fourth of the time for cooking regular brown rice. Although it doesn't have exactly the same texture, instant rice works well in this salad.

"For a festive touch, serve this slaw in radicchio or red cabbage leaves. For a creamier slaw, replace the olive oil with mayonnaise."

—minutemeals' Chef Paul

prepare the **cool tomato soup**

The green ends only of 2 scallions

2 cans (15 ounces each) diced tomatoes with mild green chiles, undrained

1 cup canned vegetable broth

2 teaspoons sugar

1/2 teaspoon ground cumin

1. Trim the white ends on both scallions and discard. Cut the green parts into 1-inch pieces.

2. Place the scallions in a blender with the undrained tomatoes, vegetable broth, sugar, and cumin. Blend until smooth. Refrigerate in the blender container until serving time.

make the **warm lemony rice, red bean, and radish slaw**

1 1/2 cups water

1 1/4 cups instant brown rice

1/2 teaspoon salt

1 can (19 ounces) red kidney beans

3 tablespoons chopped cilantro or flat-leaf parsley

2 to 4 tablespoons fresh lemon juice

3 tablespoons olive oil

Salt and pepper to taste

1 cup sliced radishes (about 4 large)

3 cups presliced cabbage

1 cup shredded carrots

1. Put the water in a medium saucepan. Cover and bring to a boil over high heat. Stir in the rice and salt and return to a boil. Reduce the heat, cover, and simmer for 10 minutes, or until tender.

2. Rinse and drain the kidney beans. Add the beans to the rice and remove the pan from the heat.

3. Chop enough cilantro or fresh parsley to measure 3 tablespoons.

4. Meanwhile, in a large bowl, with a fork, stir together the lemon juice to taste, olive oil, cilantro, and salt and pepper.

5. Trim the radishes, cut them in half and slice into half-rounds to measure 1 cup. Add to bowl, along with cabbage and carrots. Stir well to combine.

serve

1. Drain any water from the rice, add the rice to the slaw mixture, and toss until combined. Season with salt and pepper, then cover to keep warm.

2. Serve the tomato soup in 4 bowls, either as a starter or with the slaw.

3. When ready for dessert, serve the watermelon or grapes on a platter with dessert plates.

Warm Lemony Rice, Red Bean, and Radish Slaw
Single serving is 1/4 of the total recipe

CALORIES 476; PROTEIN 14g; CARBS 81g; TOTAL FAT 12g; SAT FAT 2g; CHOLESTEROL 0mg; SODIUM 531mg; FIBER 11g

spinach and brown rice casserole

italian greens with roasted red peppers

whole-wheat flatbread

honey-broiled pineapple with vanilla frozen yogurt

menu
gameplan

shopping list

Chopped scallions
(from the salad bar)

Frozen chopped spinach

Instant brown rice

Pre-shredded Cheddar cheese

Butter lettuce and radicchio blend

Sliced roasted red peppers

Pineapple slices,
fresh or frozen

Vanilla frozen yogurt

Whole-wheat or sesame flatbread

from your pantry

Garlic

Olive oil

Vegetable broth

Dried Italian herb seasoning

Salt and pepper

Extra virgin olive oil

Red wine vinegar

Honey

serves 4

beforeyoustart

Preheat the broiler.

step 1 make the **spinach and brown rice casserole**

step 2 assemble the **italian greens with roasted red peppers**

step 3 prepare the **broiled pineapple**

step 4 serve

luckyforyou

If your dried herb rack doesn't include Italian seasoning, you can improvise by making a combination of marjoram, thyme, savory, rosemary, oregano, and basil. The recipe will be perfectly happy with your own favorite herbs.

"This is great comfort food. When the family needs something soothing for dinner, turn to this menu."

—minutemeals' Chef Ruth

make the **spinach and brown rice casserole**

2 garlic cloves

1 tablespoon olive oil

1 cup chopped scallions

1 can (14$\frac{1}{2}$ ounces) vegetable broth

$\frac{1}{2}$ cup water

1 package (10 ounces) frozen chopped spinach

1 teaspoon dried Italian herb seasoning

2 cups instant brown rice

Salt and pepper to taste

2 cups (8 ounces) pre-shredded Cheddar cheese

1. Finely chop the garlic.

2. Heat the olive oil in a large deep nonstick skillet over medium-high heat until hot. Add the garlic and scallions and cook, stirring, until tender but not browned.

3. Add the vegetable broth, water, spinach, and Italian seasoning. Bring to a boil over high heat, covered, stirring to break up the spinach.

4. Stir in the rice. Cover and simmer for 5 minutes. Turn off the heat and let stand, covered, for 5 minutes. Season lightly with salt and pepper.

5. Sprinkle with the Cheddar; cover, and let stand about 2 minutes, until the cheese melts.

assemble the **italian greens with roasted red peppers**

1 bag (about 7 ounces) butter lettuce and radicchio blend

$\frac{1}{2}$ cup drained sliced jarred roasted red peppers

2 tablespoons extra virgin olive oil

1 tablespoon red wine vinegar

$\frac{1}{4}$ teaspoon salt

Pepper to taste

Put the lettuce in a large salad bowl. Add the roasted red peppers. Drizzle with oil and vinegar, add the salt, and season with pepper. Toss to coat. Place the salad bowl on the table.

prepare the **honey-broiled pineapple with vanilla frozen yogurt**

8 slices of fresh or drained canned pineapple

8 teaspoons honey

Vanilla frozen yogurt for serving

1. Preheat the broiler. Line a jelly-roll pan with aluminum foil. Arrange the pineapple slices in a single layer on the prepared pan and drizzle each slice with 1 teaspoon honey.

2. At dessert time, broil the pineapple, 4 to 5 inches from the heat, until the honey is lightly bubbling.

serve

1. Serve the rice casserole directly from the pan in which it cooked.

2. Place the flatbreads in a napkin-lined basket to serve with the casserole and salad.

3. When ready for dessert, broil the pineapple as directed above, transfer 2 slices to each of 4 dessert bowls and top with frozen yogurt. Serve while still warm.

Spinach and Brown Rice Casserole
Single serving is $\frac{1}{4}$ of the total recipe

CALORIES 465; PROTEIN 22g; CARBS 42g; TOTAL FAT 25g; SAT FAT 12g; CHOLESTEROL 59mg; SODIUM 855mg; FIBER 5g

stir-fried rice
with tofu
steamed broccolini with orange dressing
watermelon or pineapple chunks and fortune cookies

shopping list

Broccolini or broccoli florets

Stir-fry sauce

Scallions

Red peppers

Frozen peas

Firm tofu

Fresh bean sprouts

Precut watermelon or pineapple chunks (from the salad bar or the produce department)

Fortune cookies

from your pantry

Orange juice

Cornstarch

Peanut or vegetable oil

Leftover cooked brown or white rice

Lite soy sauce

serves 4

step **1** cook the **steamed broccolini with orange dressing**

step **2** make the **stir-fried rice with tofu**

step **3** **serve**

headsup

Do some advance planning to save yourself time: Make a meal with rice the day before and double up on the rice. Or buy cooked rice on the way home from the Chinese take-out. If neither of those is an option, cook up some instant brown rice. It cooks in 10 minutes.

"Broccolini is the perfect vegetable for the harried cook. Since the stems are tender, there's no peeling involved." —minutemeals' Chef Paul

cook the **steamed broccoli with orange dressing**

1 bunch broccolini or
3 cups broccoli florets

3/4 cup orange juice

1 tablespoon stir-fry sauce

2 teaspoons cornstarch

1. Bring 1 inch of water to a boil, covered, in a large saucepan. Cut the broccolini into 3-inch lengths, place in a steamer basket, and cover. Steam for 3 minutes, or just until tender-crisp.

2. Meanwhile, in a small saucepan, stir together the orange juice, stir-fry sauce, and cornstarch until the cornstarch is dissolved. Bring to a simmer over medium heat, stirring constantly. Cook for 30 seconds, or until thickened. Remove from the heat.

make the **stir-fried rice with tofu**

4 scallions

2 red peppers

1 tablespoon peanut or vegetable oil

3 cups leftover cooked brown or white rice

1 package (10 ounces) frozen peas

8 ounces firm tofu
(2 cups cubed)

2 cups fresh bean sprouts

1/3 cup stir-fry sauce

2 tablespoons lite soy sauce

1. Slice the scallions diagonally. Thinly slice the peppers.

2. Heat the peanut oil in a wok or nonstick Dutch oven over high heat. Add the scallions and peppers and cook, stirring, for 2 minutes. Add the rice and peas and cook, stirring, for 4 to 5 minutes, or until the rice is heated through.

3. Meanwhile, cube the tofu.

4. Add the tofu, bean sprouts, stir-fry sauce, and soy sauce to the wok and cook, tossing gently, for about 1 minute, or until heated through. Remove the pan from the heat.

serve

1. Ladle the rice into bowls and serve at once.

2. Divide broccolini among 4 small bowls and top each serving with some of the orange sauce.

3. When ready for dessert, divide watermelon or pineapple among 4 dessert bowls and garnish each serving with a fortune cookie. Serve with additional cookies, if desired.

Stir-Fried Rice with Tofu
Single serving is 1/4 of the total recipe
CALORIES 325; PROTEIN 14g; CARBS 50g;
TOTAL FAT 8g; SAT FAT 1g; CHOLESTEROL 0mg;
SODIUM 1202mg; FIBER 6g